Life in the Fish Bowl

Life in the Fish Bowl

F. Belton Joyner Jr.

EVERYDAY CHALLENGES OF PASTORS AND THEIR FAMILIES

Abingdon Press / *Nashville*

Life in the Fish Bowl:
Everyday Challenges for Pastors and Their Families

Copyright © 2006 by Abingdon Press

All rights reserved.

This book is printed on recycled, acid-free, elemental-chlorine-free paper.

Library of Congress Cataloging-in-Publication Data

Joyner, F. Belton
  Life in the fish bowl : everyday challenges of pastors and their families / F. Belton Joyner, Jr.
    p. cm.
  Includes bibliographical references (p.   ).
  ISBN 0-687-33294-X (binding: pbk. : alk. paper)
  1. Clergy—Family relationships.   2. Families of clergy.   I. Title.

BV4396.J69 2006
253'.22—dc22

                                                                                2006006125

06 07 08 09 10 11 12 13 14 15—10 9 8 7 6 5 4 3 2 1

MANUFACTURED IN THE UNITED STATES OF AMERICA

For Belton III,

whom I love, admire, trust, and respect

You are evidence that a child of the parsonage can turn out OK!

CONTENTS

INTRODUCTION

Some call it a parsonage. Some call it a manse. Some call it a pastorium. Some call it a rectory. Some call it home.

This book is about life in, around (sometimes under), and about the parsonage. What is it like to live in a house owned by the people who pay your salary? What is it like to have no choice but to move into a particular house whose owner says you can't bring with you your twelve-year-old cat, Oscar?[1] (Pay attention to those little numbers for the notes. Check them out; there is high-quality personal professional pastoral persiflage[2] in those notes!) What is it like to be a child growing up with the social expectation that you will be religious because "you live in the parsonage"?

And what is it like to have new friends show up on the day you move in to help you with the heavy boxes? And what is it like to have welcoming food provided for your first week because, "Pastor, you've got too much else to do"? And what is it like to be freed of the pressures and vagaries of home ownership?

There are pluses and minuses in parsonage life. (I'm going to use the term "parsonage" to represent all of those church-owned facilities in which clergy families are expected to live.) In these pages, I hope to explore this parsonage system of housing: How did it come to be? How can a pastor survive in it? What are its pitfalls? What are its "hooray" moments? What are its horror stories? What are its victories? How can you raise a family in it? What cautions will help the pastor and congregation? How does it support ministry? How can it be a means of the grace of Jesus Christ? (Oh, yes, as long as I am at it, why don't I also develop plans for peace in the Middle East, resolve conflict over stem cell research, and announce the winner of the 2010 World Series!)

Indeed, I have some trepidation in writing this book. There is no magic formula, so I cannot provide one. There are always exceptions, so I cannot foresee every circumstance. There are two sides to every coin, so I cannot always make it heads or tails. Having said that, let me offer these pages as part of a conversation. What would I say to a pastor friend about life in a parsonage? What would I want to say to a congregation who genuinely wants its parsonage "to work" for its pastor? That will be the spirit of my reflections.

Until I retired in 2001, I lived all of my life either in church-owned or school-owned housing.[3] Well, I suppose I was not living in a parsonage those four days when I had my tonsils out at the hospital in Lumberton, the overnight in the Siler City hospital when I had a mole removed, and four months in the Annapolis hospital, recovering from an automobile accident. And camp. And sleepovers. And grandparents. (You get the idea: until recently, my home base has always been a parsonage or campus housing.) That's eighteen houses (plus dorms and much fine cattle).[4]

Parsonage life has changed over the years, usually for the better. The good old days? One pastor tells of his children playing a version of tiddly-winks by dropping coins through holes in the second level flooring into a can that rested on the first floor. The good old days? In a tradition in which pastors moved frequently, early parsonages were totally furnished, right down to pots, pans, silverware, bed linens, and frequently, pious art-work.[5] Personal tastes of the parsonage family were a non-issue. More than one account has emerged of snakes in varying stages of life appearing in toilets (both the flush and the non-flush type), storage boxes, and study filing cabinets.[6]

In spite of improvements (denominational parsonage standards have helped), the bottom-line question seems to be: How do I live in a house not of my choosing in a neighborhood not of my choosing often in a town not of my choosing,[7] a house owned (and often furnished) by the same people who sign my monthly check? Just how much control should these others have over my life: my living arrangements and my livelihood? Their house. My home.

Many non-pastoral families live in rented apartments or houses. They too have limitations put upon their use of the place, but, unless hamstrung by drastic financial circumstances, they almost always have the option of moving somewhere else. A parsonage family does not have that option (at least not without the potential of great cost to pastoral relationships). American Sign Language has captured the close tie between the congregation and the abode provided for the pastor; in ASL, the word for "parsonage" simply combines the words for "church" and "house."

Housing for clergy has roots in the distant past. An Old Testament priest might live in the temple (1 Samuel 2:11 and 1 Samuel 3:2, for example). The itinerant apostles of the early church were provided places to stay as they moved around (Acts 9:43, Acts 18:2-3, Philemon 22, for example). Monasteries and convents were built for those clergy who became monks or nuns; the monastic movement was flourishing within four centuries after Pentecost. Special housing for religious leaders was built; the first papal residence was probably built in the fifth century. By the sixth century, a parish system was fully developed (numerous separate congregations, each with its own priest). Wealthy landowners would build churches on their property and would insist on the right to choose the priest. Housing for the resident priest was then provided by the landowner. (There seems to be no record as to whether the landowner decided which pictures to hang on the walls and whether the carpet was all sea-foam green.[8])

In England, the benefice (recognize the word "benefit"?) provided some clergy an endowment and residential privileges, often without any particular regard to the quality or frequency of the pastoral work. The key figure in Methodism's early days, John Wesley, grew up in the parsonage for St. Andrews Church in Epworth, Lincolnshire, in northeastern England. That rectory was often the target of parishioners and townspeople who were less than thrilled with the public life of John Wesley's father, Samuel. Part of the arrangement in that parish was that the land between the parsonage and the church was available for the rector to cultivate. When his congregation got fed up with him, some of them would simply burn the good reverend's crops. And occasionally, his house. (And you thought it was bad when the chair of the parsonage committee picked out a wallpaper you didn't like!)

One of the stories that floats through Methodist circles is how five-year-old John Wesley was rescued by a human ladder when the Epworth parsonage burned to the ground in 1709. This incident had a great impact on Wesley, who viewed himself as "a brand plucked from the burning," no doubt saved by God for some meaningful purpose. (These days, it is not recommended that we burn down the crops or the house of anyone who might need a nudge to hear God's call to ministry. Perhaps, instead of fire, it would be sufficient to encourage what Wesleyans call "a strangely warmed heart.")

The earliest preachers in America were mostly circuit riders, men who went from place to place, never establishing any one place as home. Francis Asbury, one of the first Methodist bishops, dreaded the day when those firebrand preachers would want to settle down. The early Methodist Episcopal *Book of Discipline* enjoined preachers not even to consider getting married without consulting with preacher colleagues. But hormones and love and urban life being what they are, there soon developed a pattern of "located preachers," those who served in one place, perhaps even with just one congregation (and, presumably, with just one wife).

In a pastoral assignment system in which a new pastor moves in the same day as the former pastor moves out, there is an advantage (for church and pastor) in having housing as a non-issue; ergo, the parsonage. The parsonage is for the benefit of the pastoral appointment. It is not to be thought of as pastoral compensation.[9] Why is that the case? This question was answered in 1988 (at least, for United Methodists) with this statement in *The Book of Discipline 1988*: "Housing shall not be considered as part of compensation or remuneration, but shall be considered as a means provided by the local church, and for the convenience of the local church, to enable its ministry and the itinerant ministry of the Annual Conference."[10]

Parsonage questions usually boil down to this one matter: Does it enable the ministry of Jesus Christ? Serious ego and unbending habit and conflicting mission and financial pressures and differing values all blend and blur to make this a difficult question to answer. Nevertheless, it is a good question to keep in mind.

The word "parsonage" grows out of the word "parson." The word "parson," in turn, comes from the Latin *persona*, which means "person." During the Middle Ages, the *parson* was the *person* in the village who could read, write, sign documents, make things official, and generally cause or prevent most of community life. I am intrigued that the word "parsonage"[11] has its roots in the centrality of the pastor (the parson) in the life of the parish. Changing views toward the parsonage may in some measure reflect changing attitudes toward the importance of the pastoral role.

Throughout these pages, there are stories and memories, all purported to be true. (Truth is in the eye, ear, nose, and throat of the beholder.) When friends have given me their accounts of parsonage life, I have agreed to disguise locale and personalities. This approach protects both the innocent and the guilty! I am grateful for those who, when learning of this project, regaled me with descriptions of chartreuse walls, of the distribution of parsonage keys throughout the community, of water freezing in an inside toilet, and of a parsonage condemned by the city because of toxic mold. And there were stories of a refrigerator filled with good food on moving day; of new furniture replacing shabby hand-me-downs; of caring, unobtrusive visits by church members who wanted things to be right; and of wise planning for brand-new parsonages.

Let me hasten to say to the good folks in Faison, Chadbourn, Fairmont, Siler City, Wilmington, Bahama, Raleigh, Mebane, and Durham, I have nothing but love and appreciation for how we have done parsonage together. Maybe there is a clue in that: doing parsonage together (church and pastor and family) goes a long way toward letting this system of care and support become an instrument of ministry in the name of Jesus Christ.

SOMEONE ELSE'S HOUSE

Three-year-old Erika and her two-year-old brother, Ben, were having a good splash in the parsonage bathtub. Their mother had stepped out for a moment, leaving the children to push rubber ducks, play with soap bubbles, and see how high the plastic ball would bounce if held under water for a few seconds. Mom got back just in time to see Ben exuberantly throw a cupful of water toward the ceiling. She heard Erika's chastisement of the younger sibling: "Don't do that, Ben; the Methodists won't like it!"

Yep. It does not take long to learn that the parsonage family is living in a house owned by someone else.[1] For some pastors, this is a matter of great relief ("It's not my problem if the hot water heater goes out") and to other pastors it is a matter of considerable threat ("How can I build up any equity for a retirement home?"). Many people live in houses and apartments they do not own, but at some level, financial considerations being equal, they do so by choice. For some parsonage families, having to live in someone else's house can stir the kind of resentment that comes from continued feelings of dependence and lack of control.

Often, the sense of "whose house is it" is symbolized by how many people have keys to the parsonage. The pastor? The pastor's spouse? The pastor's children? A neighbor? Chair of the trustees? Chair of the parsonage committee? Chair of the task force to decide what new bedroom furniture to buy? Former chair of the trustees? Former chair of the parsonage committee? Former chair of the decorating committee? How about the former pastor? The former pastor's spouse? The former pastor's children? The pastor's second cousin twice removed by marriage? (Just how many cousins get removed by marriage?)

The possibilities are immense, and the uncertainty of "whose house is it" can be magnified by the immense and uncertain list of people who have a key! My suggestion is to make a list of everyone who has a key. This arrangement should make for fewer surprises. If the barn door is already open, so to speak, maybe a change of locks is called for, with a new list made of all key holders. Why do they need a key? When do they need a key? How can non-key holders obtain a key when necessary? Who knows who has a key? How about borrowers of a parsonage key signing out the key and signing in its return? Does the pastor agree to the key policy?

It is not always nosiness that leads to "key abuse." Sometimes it is a good kind of pride. One pastor tells of living in a brand-new parsonage. The church members were rightfully proud of the work they had done to create a good living space for the pastor and his family. In fact, if the pastor was home, it was not unusual for someone to knock at the door and ask if they could show visitors around the house. (See chapter 6 on visitors!) On one occasion, the pastor's wife was gone and the pastor's car was in the shop, so, to all appearances, no one was at home. The across-the-street neighbors were members of the church, and one of them, being a church officer, had a key to the parsonage. Wanting to show the new house to some visiting relatives, the neighbor used the key. ("I know they won't mind my showing this beautiful house to my kin people.") All seemed to go well during the short tour. The touring ladies were surprised at just how lovely the house had been prepared, but that did not match their surprise when they stepped into the bedroom and found the pastor standing totally nude in the middle of the floor, having just stepped out of the shower. (I was not there, but perhaps if the brother had quickly assumed the posture of Michelangelo's statue *David*, the visitors would have thought he was another bit of religious artwork.)

Most congregations understand that although the parsonage is their real estate, it is the home of pastor and family.[2] Typically, the church knows that it is the church's house but is the pastor's home. Misunderstanding can occur. One area in which this tension can become expensive is insurance. Some pastors assume that because the parsonage belongs to the church, the church's property insurance will cover the loss of the pastor's personal items that are in the parsonage. Not so![3] (If you are a pastor living in a parsonage and do not have your own insurance on your personal property, put this book down and run to the nearest insurance agency and buy some renter's insurance. Such coverage is relatively inexpensive but invaluable. Of course, be sure to put a bookmark in these pages and leave the book where you can find it. You might consider hiding it, because no doubt others are clamoring to get their hands on this work of literature. Tell them to go to the bookstore and buy their own.)

While you are at it, make sure the personal coverage you buy includes any property you keep at the church (books, computer, robe, stoles, chalice, artwork, old Ping Pong balls, used toothpicks, exercise clothes—give me a break; I don't know what you keep at the church.) If you are a friendly layperson (or even if you are unfriendly), make sure your pastor understands that the local church's insurance is for the local church's property, not the pastor's property. This is not because the local church is mean, but because that is the way insurance works.[4]

Guess what. Because the congregation owns the parsonage, the pastor does not get to keep the house when she retires! This seemingly obvious observation may escape the planning and attention of both pastor and people. (Of course, some pastors are also people.) In setting pastoral compensation, a finance committee might be heard muttering, "We don't need to pay the preacher so much because we provide a house; there is no housing expense for our pastor, so there is less need for salary money." After living in parsonage after parsonage, a cleric might well ponder, "This is a grand arrangement. There is no housing cost for me, so I can spend my money on my collection of portraits of John Calvin." Neither such muttering nor such pondering is wise, practical, or good stewardship.

When the Reverend Ms. McAllister is ready to retire after forty-three years of active pastoring, where is she going to live? Her grandparents long ago sold the family farm. Her brother Egbert has a houseful of children. The Smiling Face Retirement Community has a waiting list of fourteen years. Low-income rental housing does not seem to be an attractive option. Her camping tent has developed a leak. Where is she going to move as her replacement pastor moves into the parsonage?[5]

Congregations, in setting pastoral salary, and pastors, in spending pastoral income, need to allow for the pastor's retirement home. A congregation is not likely to want to buy two houses at once—(a) a parsonage and (b) a retirement home for the pastor—but it does need to take into account the fact that the pastor is gaining no equity in the parsonage. Salary level needs to be generous enough for the pastor to set aside some funds for future housing needs (buying a house, making safe investments, giving the author of this book large sums of money in the hopes that Toni and I can let you use our spare bedroom). On the balancing side, the pastor should set aside a portion of income for future housing, not anticipating that "something will work out."

Clearly, pastors in low-income settings find it difficult, if not impossible, to make provisions for retirement housing. Denominational leaders, congregation officials, and pastors need to form a team to address this concern. Leaving future living arrangements unattended creates personal hardship, connectional disharmony, and local church dismay.

It is not necessary that a pastor's retirement home be paid for at the end of one's active ministry. In fact, there is a school of thought that argues that it is better not to have the house paid for. There are tax advantages to having interest payments and, for the pastor, tax advantages to having mortgage payments.[6] In planning the final years of pastoring, clergy need to anticipate whether they will rent, buy, build, or move in with the chairperson of the church council.[7]

What really irritates some clergy about living in a parsonage is that choices about furniture and accessories and color schemes rest in the hands of others. (Traditions about how much of a parsonage is to be furnished vary from denomination to denomination and from locale to locale. In some places, the parsonage is simply an empty house. In other settings, everything is provided except den furniture and bedroom items. Most parsonages have the major appliances.)[8]

Speaking of major appliances (did you note the smooth transition?), one colleague told of mentioning to the church trustee chair that there was no light in the parsonage refrigerator. Without missing a beat, the chairperson said, "Oh, don't even worry about replacing the bulb. Since the door won't shut all the way, that light just burns out too fast anyway."

Clearly, it is important that congregation and pastor have common understandings about issues around the parsonage. The best time for coming to these agreements is before moving day! In some polities, there is an introductory visit of the new pastor with local church officials. In other patterns, there is a search committee with whom these discussions might take place. A number of questions might be addressed: If there is duplication of furniture, whose furniture gets stored? Where? Who pays for the storage? What time will the house be available on moving day? How have pets been received in this parsonage? Who pays for cable or satellite hook-up for television? A congregation would want to know of the pastor: What help will you need when you move? Can we provide meals on moving day? How many people will be with you? If there is an oil tank, who is responsible for having it filled on moving day? (Departing pastor? New pastor? Congregation?).[9] Do you prefer a utilities allowance or having utility bills sent to the church? (That judgment might well be made already in denominational policy.) How will moving expenses be handled? (Again, some churches have these matters as part of stated guidelines.)

Both pastor and congregation can benefit from an early conversation about the history of the parsonage. Sensitive listening might reveal things that have been problematic in the past ("We decided not to build next door to the church in order to give the pastor some privacy"), areas of particular caution ("Ha-ha! We had one preacher who never cut the grass!"), matters of genuine pride ("Those boxwoods were imported from East Magellan"), and things open for decision ("Some pastors put their garbage out with the church's trash and some don't; it doesn't matter."). A pastor would do well to hear the story behind the story as the congregational representatives tell how the parsonage came to be. A parsonage committee member would be helpful if she or he noted when the new pastor seemed a bit flummoxed by something the church takes for granted.[10]

Of course, getting to walk around in the parsonage will help the new pastor and family begin to understand their new home setting. The cooperation of the pastor who might still be in the parsonage will be needed to arrange such a visit. (The pastor who is leaving will—it is hoped—be pleasantly absent, having of, course, OK'd the "tour." There is a tension between a pastor's forewarning another and a pastor's creating a self-fulfilling prophecy for another.)

Pastors who chafe at the parsonage system can re-examine the basic question: What makes most probable the ministry of Jesus Christ? My preferences and my pride need to take second place to that core question. There are tensions among the covenants clergy have made: ordination covenants, marriage covenants, baptismal covenants, family covenants. In each case, it is easy to confuse my wishes for the will of God. (If I look into the biblical mirror, does Jesus look a lot like me? My tastes? My values? My desires?)

There is more to be said about making my home in someone else's house. Home is more than house. The rest of this book will include some more thinking about how a parsonage can be a home.

CHAPTER 2

FIRST DAY AT THE PARSONAGE

B rad Graham proudly drove the rented truck down the rural highway. He was on his way to his first pastoral assignment. As he
looked ahead and saw the parsonage, he smiled. Several members
of the congregation were there, waiting to help. The district superintendent was there, ready to greet the new colleague.[1] It was a moment to be
remembered and cherished for years to come: my first appointment, my
first parsonage, my first chance to be among "my people."

Brad pulled to a stop just past the driveway. Thankful that he had prac-
ticed backing with those big side mirrors, he slipped the moving truck
into reverse and began slowly to bring his worldly goods to their new
home. The big truck inched back toward the carport, where the unloading would take place. With genuine affection for his new congregation,
Brad threw a hand of greeting to the waiting throng, eager to get to know
the new pastor.

"Welcome!" they exclaimed with heartfelt enthusiasm. Four more feet
to the carport. Three more feet to the carport. Two more feet to the carport. And then with a resounding crash, multiplied by the sound of tum-
bling rafters and broken bricks, Brad and his truck completed their
journey, having just torn the parsonage carport from its accustomed place
next to the parsonage.

Not bad. Several thousand dollars worth of damage to the parsonage as
the pastor moves in![2] What a wonderful first impression!

First impressions are funny things. Who knows what "glasses" folks will
be wearing when they first look at one another! A trustee might be
remembering a former pastor who left without paying bills. Another
member might be recalling the self-promise never to get close to another
pastor because it hurts so much when they leave. A pastor might be
thinking of how he had promised his wife that this house would be better than the last one. Another pastor is pondering how she will let the
children know it will not be safe to play in the yard. A member of the parsonage committee could be hoping the pastor's family will say something
nice about the new living room sofa. Did the pastor rent a truck or pay
for a moving van?[3] My, how did the preacher afford such a nice car? Or,

does our new pastor expect to lead funeral processions in that old trap?

Ah, first impressions! Everyone wants to be on good behavior, but naturally each is curious about the other.

It is not only the church members who are curious about the pastor, but also the next-door neighbors. These folks might or might not be members of the congregation. If they have been living next to the parsonage very long, they probably have gotten used to the comings and goings of clergy families (and learned that the pastor is human enough to wear shorts when mowing the lawn). Neighbors might even have heard a bit of, uh, family exchanges as spouses decide the finer things of daily life: whose turn it is to pick up the children, why the garbage did not get to the road in time for pick-up, who left on all the outside lights for four days as well as nights, and just how long the in-laws are going to stay when they descend on the household next week.

The neighbors have a good insight into the truism that pastors are only human. Some guard those insights with integrity; some use those insights as currency in community gossip games; some hardly give it a thought.

All of this is to say that on the first day the pastor might take the time to greet the next-door neighbor. Five minutes is all it would take to say, "I'm your new neighbor at the parsonage. Keep your stinking nose out of my business." (You probably would want to rephrase that last part to something like, "I look forward to getting to know you.") Some neighbors enjoy being next to the parsonage; some find it a non-issue; some wish "those religious freaks next door" would leave them alone. A pastor's family will be known as the pastor's family.[4] For better or worse, that is a reality that shapes neighborhood life. (More on this in chapters ahead.)

On the first day at the parsonage, sometimes there can be more "help" than is desired! More than one clergy family can give an account of a friendly (aggressively friendly?) welcomer who not only helps bring boxes in from the moving truck but who also "helps" by putting the family's personal items onto shelves and into drawers. There are two net effects of this practice: (a) the family has little notion where needed items might be and (b) the helper has a quick survey of the family's belongings. In most cases, the volunteer aide will ask before beginning this unpacking. (Can you practice saying, "No, thank you. We packed a certain way and I guess we'll have to unpack in a certain way in order to find things! But would you help me decide where I might put these pet tarantulas?")[5]

If previous arrangements have not been made, try to make connections with the power company, the gas company, the telephone company, and any other utilities services. If the billing has been in the name of your predecessor, this first day is the first day to get that changed! (Most utilities can be advised in advance of a switch-over date.) There is some wisdom in having utility bills in the name of the church even if they are paid by the pastor. This makes the transition go more smoothly, although the departing and the arriving colleagues need to be clear on who pays which portion of the month's billing.[6]

On the first day at the parsonage, there could be a few persons who show up to score early points with the pastor. (A genuine desire to help motivates almost all of those who come.) If the conversation begins to shift from "This surely is a hot day for moving" to "You know, Brother Turkey[7] never did seem to understand the importance of playing softball with the youth," the incoming pastor would do well to make a mental note about softball and throw the conversation back to the weather. There will be plenty of time for the pastor to get caught up in the usual surfeit of church arguments, so the first day is not the best setting for triangulation.[8]

In a retirement speech, one pastor told this story about the first day at a parsonage. (He was an honorable man given to telling the truth.) During the humid and dirty part of the afternoon, boxes were, of course, still stacked in every corner of the house. Husband and wife were exhausted from both the emotional shifting of gears and the physical stress of unloading. All the helpers had left and the couple faced the arduous task of finding where they had packed bedroom slippers, which box contained the alarm clock, and what surprises lurked in containers labeled "miscellaneous."[9] About to collapse from exhaustion, they heard the doorbell signal the arrival of a visitor. It was a member of the parsonage committee. She wore a hat and white gloves. This was clearly a social call of the first order! Duty answered the door and invited the good sister into the parsonage. A bit aghast at the realities of moving day, the visitor said, "I just wanted to welcome you and to see if there is anything I can do." With that, she took her gloved hand and swept it across the top of the door frame. Glancing at her glove, the caller said with serious sympathy, "I can see, my dear, that you have not had time to do your dusting."

The retiring pastor completed the account by saying that before he left that appointment, he could not help a slight smile as he said over that woman, "Dust to dust. . . ."

The truth is that most assistance on moving day is careful, practical, and appreciated. Often, congregations will prepare food not only for the first day but for the first week. Although it might be a good change of pace to get out of the house on moving day, most families would prefer to eat in their new home and not have to get cleaned up for a "public viewing." Will food be provided for professional movers as well as the pastoral family? (Some movers value this hospitality; some might prefer a break away from the chores; it doesn't hurt to ask!) It helps if the congregation has checked out the dietary preferences and needs of the parsonage family. It also helps if these early meals come in containers that do not have to be returned! One church made a point of not labeling who sent what. In that way the new pastor could extend a generic thank you and not have to track down a dozen folks or so. ("Here is your plastic bowl, Ms. Jones; thank you so much for the purple cottage cheese.")

Early days in a parsonage can become a time to learn favorite foods of the new community. (What is that green stuff in the gelatin mold? It turns out to be what the Perkinses bring to every covered-dish supper: tuna pistachio surprise. Everyone loves it, but it does look a bit intimidating at an initial glance into the parsonage refrigerator.) The wife of one pastor celebrated the fresh bread and fresh vegetables that showed up at their coastal parsonage. What she did not celebrate—at first, anyhow—was the local delicacy, crabs. A fisherman showed up with a bushel basket of crabs. She thanked him with as much energy as her surprise could generate; he left the basket on the washing machine in the corner of the kitchen.

When her husband came in from an afternoon of get-acquainted visits, she told him about the crabs. He rushed to see the generous gift and discovered an empty container. The crabs had conducted their own exploration of the parsonage and were behind the washer, on the kitchen cabinets, behind the door, and in other places of mystery. Coming from way inland and not being accustomed to the ways of crabbing, she reports that she mounted her defense by climbing onto a chair. Although her shaking might have seemed to be brought on by religious ecstasy, it did not seem to stop until loving husband had found all those crabs and returned them to the basket. (At least, they hoped he found all of the visiting crustaceans! Although this story is not from my family, even as I typed these words I found myself looking under the desk for a possible escaped mutant crab. Would that make a good movie?)

Even with the best of intent, it is possible for the move not to take place on the planned-for day (or at least not at the planned-for hour). In a system such as United Methodist polity, all moves have to be coordinated because the moves all take place on the same designated day.[10] It is a hazard to be on highways on United Methodist moving day! Certainly, in the cases of retirement or moves to non-local church assignment or major renovation in the parsonage or a major shortage of liquor boxes in town,[11] the new parsonage family might be delayed. Make sure everyone is in the loop when this happens. (Some congregations offer to pay for motel accommodations or other temporary arrangements.)

Another kind of "first day at the parsonage" occurs when a previously single pastor gets married. Although the Reverend Ms. Armistead may have lived in the parsonage for two years, it is "first day" for her newly minted husband, Howard.

One pastor's wife told me of everything that happened on the day she moved into the parsonage with her student pastor husband. He had lived there before they married so now she came to join him in the trailer that served as parsonage.[12] These events all unfolded on her first day as a new bride in her new parsonage home: (1) She did not feel well in the shower and did not know why. Later when her husband showered, he screamed. It turns out that the ungrounded shower was a conduit for electricity. (2) Trying to heat water for a cup of coffee, she managed to create a great, leaping flame on the gas stove, thus discovering that there were no controls on the stove. (3) She tripped on a broken step as she exited the trailer to go to a "welcome" party at the home of an affluent member. The resulting scraping of skin ran all the way down her back. (4) Her husband and she attended the elegant welcome party. (5) Back at the trailer, the temperature was 14 degrees F, because the oil heat had gone out. (6) The couple asked the hosts of the party if they might return for the evening's rest. (7) At 2:00 A.M., their hosts offered them boiled chitlins[13] as a snack. (8) At 4:00 A.M. the couple trundled off for what sleep might remain in the evening. (9) At 6:00 A.M., a knock on the door told the pastor and wife that breakfast was ready. (10) The pastor, not having been to bed because he still had a sermon to prepare, was greeted with the news that their hosts had fixed a breakfast of brains and eggs. (11) Then it was off to church and a chance for the congregation to meet the pastor's bride. (12) Gasp.

Now, having read that, don't you feel better about your first day at the parsonage?

CHAPTER 3

GOLDFISH AND PREACHERS

Someone has said[1] that living in a parsonage is like living in a goldfish bowl. Truth to tell, I have never felt that way, but enough "someones" have said it for me to recognize that for many parsonage families it is true.

One colleague said he got up at 3:00 A.M. to go to the bathroom. The phone rang. It was a neighbor to the parsonage. "I saw the light go on in your bathroom," she said, "and wanted to make sure that you are all right." When assured that everything was OK, the caller went on, "Well, as long as you are up, is this a good time to talk?"

By the nature of ministry, clergy are public persons. They stand in front of groups and speak. They go into hospitals and know their way around. They are recognized in malls by persons they do not remember. They are known (at least in a small town) by Presbyterians, United Methodists, Episcopalians, Pentecostals, Quakers, Two-Seed-in-the-Spirit-Predestinarian-Baptists, Disciples, Roman Catholics, and many people who are not Christian in belief and/or practice. Clergy become the chaplains of civic clubs.[2] Clergy pray at all kinds of community events (parades, store openings, NASCAR races, installations of officials, dedications of parks).[3] Clergy who wear clerical collars are instantly identified.

In light of all this "public persona," is it any wonder that for the pastor the rhythm of life needs to include some "off duty" private time? Vacation days are days to be protected.[4] And time at home at the parsonage needs to be "down" time. Without the recharging of the batteries, the pastor is likely to burn out very quickly. The parsonage does not need to be yet another place of public display.

Most church members understand the pastor's need for "home time." They are not likely to show up unannounced (unless that is a community pattern of friendship). But passers-by might notice what is going on at the parsonage. One clergy spouse tells of mowing the grass on a very hot summer day. The parsonage was on a busy corner across the street from the church. When people stopped at the corner stop sign late at night, they often tossed beer cans out car windows. This meant that whoever was mowing the lawn had to pick up these discards and toss them into the parsonage trash. After several such trips to the garbage can, this spouse gathered up yet one more of the offending cans and rather than running it to the trash, held the empty in hand as the mowing continued.

It was only when a couple of cars stopped at the corner that this pastor's wife realized the impression she gave: parading in front of the parsonage, beer can in hand. On the next Sunday, she found out who had been in one of those curious cars. One of the church officers was busy telling another about seeing the pastor's wife with the beer can. "Well, anybody mowing the grass in 98-degree weather needs a beer," said the supportive member. After the explanation from the teetotaler spouse, all joined in a hearty laugh. She decided that the fish bowl could be a fun place!

If a parsonage is next door to the church building, the two facilities can sort of merge in the minds of congregation and parsonage family. Some churches have expected nearby parsonage space to be available for Sunday school classes. The parsonage has provided emergency bathroom capacity for the next-door church. There are a few parsonages that are physically connected to church buildings. Those attending church services might stroll through the parsonage yard on the way to church. This closeness can magnify any privacy tensions that might exist.

Another issue that emerges when the parsonage is next to or across the street from the church is that persons seeking help can easily spot "where the reverend lives." If there is no one at the church to assist a stranded motorist, hungry wanderer, or panicked runaway, such visitors guess that "the brick building next door" is the parsonage. A knock at the door asks that the hospitality of the church be extended by the home of the pastor. Of course, this is not necessarily a bad thing. The stranger at the door might be an angel. "Do not neglect to show hospitality to strangers, for by doing that some have entertained angels without knowing it" (Hebrews 13:2). A steady stream of such persons in need can create a tension between the servanthood ministry of the pastor and the pastor's human need for time away.[5]

When a pastoral family asks for privacy, some congregants may hear the request as a barrier. "What I want," one pastor remarked, "is not a wall; I simply want a fence, so folks have to slow down a bit before coming into my family's space!" Some families enjoy entertaining more than others do. Some clergy homes are places of constant dinners, parties, group meetings, and the like. Other clergy abodes offer none of the above. With this variety of attitudes around, pastors can understand if a church member makes a wrong assumption about the current parsonage family. ("Mr. Brown just loved to have people dropping in, so I thought you would too.")

Some parsonage families have found a happy medium about their privacy by offering an occasional open house at the parsonage. Obvious times for such hospitality are after major renovations have been done or when there is a major time of celebration (Christmas, homecoming, graduation, Ground Hog Day).[6] These settings are a joy for those pastoral households whose personalities call for a high level of relationships; the same settings are torment for those parsonage households whose personalities call for solitude. If you are the sort who finds the thought of an open house to be a threat to your well-being, don't have them! If you are the sort who finds the thought of an open house exhilarating, go for it! If you are the sort who is somewhere in between, perhaps you can co-opt a friend or two from the church to help with the planning, the food preparation, and even the hosting. (People with the spiritual gift of hospitality are not better than those without such gifts, but they surely are good to have around when you need them!)

If the parsonage is a goldfish bowl, there are always a few folks who want to jump into the water with the fish. Privacy? Home? "Reverend, we have always understood the parsonage to be an extension of the church. We enjoy holding meetings there." In response to that broad hint, one pastor replied, "The parsonage is not an extension of the church building; it is our home, home for our family."[7] Some people like to open their homes for meetings; others do not like to open their homes for meetings. Parsonage families should be free to make such choices as would any other family in the congregation.

Part of what makes any place a home (instead of a house) is the ability to have some freedom, some ease, some opportunity "just to be." The shadow side of this privacy is that parsonage homes, like some other homes, can be a place of hidden abuse and emotional chaos. Even so, the healthiest relationships and the best pastoral strengths are most likely to be nurtured and maintained in an environment when the pastoral family has some time to itself. (Another chapter will take a look at family life in the parsonage.)

Frequently, what is taken to be an invasion of pastoral privacy is merely a misguided effort to support the clergy family. One wife of a pastor tells of an unexpected parsonage visitor: "The first parsonage my husband and I lived in had been newly renovated. The congregation was very proud of the work they had done. One night while I was preparing supper, there was a knock at the door. A member of the parsonage committee had brought a member of her family to show off the improvements to the parsonage. She said, 'Don't mind us! Just keep on doing what you are doing. I'm just going to show my sister what we have done here.' I was busy frying fish and at first got embarrassed and then got angry. That night I had a little talk with myself. Which would I rather have: a parsonage committee who cares about the parsonage or a committee that does not care? I decided that I was glad they cared about the house they provided and I had to laugh about the intrusion."

Some of us would have had more than fried fish for supper that night. We probably would have chewed rather thoroughly on that interrupting member. But there is a good reminder in this account: Can I respond to the intent of the "intruder" more than I do to the action alone?

Obviously, if a constant invasion of privacy creates family strife and pastoral dysfunction, someone needs to say something to somebody! If a gentle word to the offender is not sufficient ("Hazel, it embarrasses me when people drop by when the house is such a mess. Do you mind calling me before you drop by?"), the pastor might speak to the group that helps her or him relate to the congregation. (In some churches, this is a pastor-parish relations committee; in others, it is a pastoral advisory committee; in others, it is a pastor support team.) Together, they can develop a strategy to help the congregation understand the parsonage family's need for its own space.

Having neighbors who will watch out for the parsonage can be a supportive comfort when the pastor has to be away for a long period of time. (One pastor's wife with a new baby tried to wash and dry a quick load of diapers on Sunday morning. Steam poured from the dryer vent and wafted toward the church next door. One of the members came pounding on the door, suspecting that the house was on fire.) It is simple neighborly kindness to keep an eye out for "anything out of the ordinary" at the parsonage. Does a broken window mean there has been a break-in or that the baseball game got a little vigorous? Does the heavy smoke from a usually docile chimney hint of danger or something more mundane?[8] Does the uncut grass mean the pastor has been busy or that something is amiss in the parsonage?[9] Looking into a goldfish bowl is not always done out of curiosity; sometimes we want to check on the well-being of the fish.

Some parsonages include the pastor's study. This mixture of "home" and "work" can make it difficult for the pastor to get the needed distance from the pressures and responsibilities of pastoring. Unless there is a separate outside entrance for the study, this "in home" arrangement can add stress to counseling settings ("Do I want everybody in the parsonage to know I came to see the pastor?"), can keep extra pressure on household cleaning ("We can't put those boxes there; everybody who comes to the study will see them"), and can offer the overhearing of parsonage family life as entertainment for visitors ("I hate you! I don't care if you are my sister! Mama likes you more than she does me!") Privacy is important for the pastor's study!

Goldfish bowl? Come to think of it, what do the goldfish see when they look out at us looking in at them? Perhaps they think it is great fun to watch the silly shenanigans of those human types! Perhaps they wonder who will next drop in a pellet of food. Perhaps they are bored at seeing the same thing every time they peer through the glass.

I don't know what goldfish think. But when I have looked out of the parsonage goldfish bowl, most often I have seen persons who care, persons who love Jesus Christ, and persons who are working on loving me. I like that view from the bowl.

CHAPTER 4

FAMILY FABRIC

When the bishop informed me of his intent to move me after my four happy years in a warm and accepting small town, our tenth-grader son wrote the bishop a letter. In the correspondence, our son spelled out several ways his life would be ruined by this move: friendships lost, school student government positions gone, academic achievements set aside, tennis team position wiped out, Scouting progress hindered, school band disappeared, puppet ministry ended. (The bishop replied that he still thought the move was best.)

We moved. Completely by coincidence, on our very first Sunday in the new appointment, the youth softball team from the church we were leaving was to play a game with the team from our new congregation. The game was planned long before we even knew we were moving, much less before we knew where we were going. We had not moved to our new parsonage (the practice was to go to one's new assignment immediately for the first Sunday but not to move to the new community until a week or so later). When it was time for the game, our son asked me which team he should play for: with the youth he knew and enjoyed from the church we were leaving or with the youth from our new church (his not knowing a single one of them). I left it up to him. He decided to play for the new youth group, having worshiped in that church only once and having never lived in its home city. When he decided to play for the new group, I knew he had begun the slow, difficult work of settling into new routines in a different parsonage. It's part of the life of a parsonage family.

A student pastor sent me an account of what happened when his family moved to his first assignment while in seminary. On their second night at the parsonage, they were having a family prayer time. His wife and he each took a turn saying a prayer. They thanked God for the roof over their heads and for the privilege of serving a church. They asked God to help them adjust and feel secure in their new surroundings. When it came time for their young son to pray, he offered this prayer: "God, thank you for today. Thank you for this house. And now can we move, please?" More than one family member has felt that way on moving day!

The family fabric can be put under a great deal of stress when moving from one parsonage to another. It is more than just the change from one community to another (lots of people do that all the time). Like a military family under orders, the parsonage family is told where to live. Some of the family might be thrilled; others in the family might be thrown into the doldrums; some accept that such a life is just the way it is; others lament being in such an unsettled family. In other words, family members respond in a variety of ways to being in a different parsonage.

Once the family has moved in, life in a parsonage is going to unfold as does family life in other Christian homes: good days, bad days, life-as-usual days. Perhaps in a parsonage there are more sudden emergency interruptions than most people get: ("My mother just died," "Bill has gone to the hospital," "There has been a bad wreck out on Highway 501," "My cat has appendicitis,"[1] "The church is on fire," and that all-time favorite, "I hated the hymns we sang last Sunday." In spite of national Do Not Call lists, parsonage phones seemed programmed to ring (a) at mealtime, (b) at mealtime, (c) at mealtime, or (d) during brief pastoral snoozes.

However you slice it, parsonage families are affected by the pastor's work life. The telephone rings. And rings. And rings. And rings. One colleague reports a phone going dead in the middle of a conversation; her daughter had cut the phone cord so she could have some time with Mama! Pastoral responsibilities cannot always be "left at the office."

Expectations can be put upon members of the household simply because they are in the pastor's family.[2] Does a child of the parsonage always have to be the substitute acolyte? Is the husband of the pastor expected to add a bass voice to the choir? Does the mission chairperson have only the parsonage number to call when looking for someone to lead the next mission study?

Although my observation is that congregations have slacked off in their standard expectations of members of the parsonage family, for those family members who still feel guilt and anger and disappointment over these "requests," it is no small matter. The alleged wild behavior of parsonage children (Alleged! Repeat it: alleged) could simply be an effort to throw off the burden of having outsiders define "who I am." For a spouse who senses that the congregation wanted "two for the price of one," there can be an inner struggle to maintain clarity of roles. For the single pastor, there might be an internal question: "Does the congregation think it got cheated because I am not married?"

What is the best way to handle those duty demands put upon the parsonage family?[3]

First, keep in mind that congregations often descend on all new members—parsonage family or not—to see where their gifts and energies best mesh with the church's life and mission. The early request to join the choir might well be an invitation made to all new congregants and not just to the husband of the pastor.

Second, think in advance how you might respond if asked to undertake some particularly ill suited and onerous task. Practice saying it to the mirror! ("Why, thank you, Beauregard, for asking me to bake eighteen dozen cookies for the Vacation Bible School, but I fear the health department would close down the church if word got out that I had cooked anything for public consumption!")[4]

Third, keep a good sense of humor.[5] The persons who ask your daughter to stay in the nursery for six weeks in a row may simply be trying to help your daughter feel at home at the new church. A good, pleasant spirit will go a long way to defusing any notion that the parsonage family is too (lazy, bored, unspiritual, mean, selfish) to help out at church.

Fourth, do find places where your gifts can be part of the congregation's life. You have no more—or less—responsibility for such involvement than other members. If your personal ministry is low-key, so be it! If your personal ministry is listening, so be it! If your personal ministry is teaching, so be it! If your personal ministry is loving your spouse, so be it! If your personal ministry is parenting your children, so be it!

Fifth, go ahead and do whatever is asked of you. (I do not recommend that you intentionally do it poorly in the hopes that the demands will die down.) You might find new joy in something you have not tried before. (Of course, you might also find fresh agony in something you have not tried before.)

Some clergy families see themselves as a team ministry. That is fine. (Be aware of the problems that can occur when there is a blurring of the pastoral role.) A parsonage family can be alert to the possibility that their "up to the eyeballs" involvement in everything at the church might be blocking the emergence of other leaders in the congregation. And it can be a bit tough on successor pastoral families!

Bottom line: be yourself and be the person you are becoming in Christ Jesus.

One family issue for some parsonage households is schooling for the children. Public schools? Private schools? Home schooling? There is not a one-size-fits-all answer. What is the nature of the local school system? What is the mission of the private school? What gains and losses will there be in home schooling? If a pastor's children are not in the same school situation as most of the children in a congregation, subtle tensions can develop in the congregation. ("Is her child too good to go to P.S. 310?" "What kind of social statement is the preacher trying to make by keeping his son at a low-performing high school?" "I think we ought to support public education, so why is it all right for the pastor's children to do home schooling?") Although school decisions are family matters, there might be some wisdom in sharing with the pastoral advisory group the rationale for schooling choices.[6]

People are not the only ingredients in some parsonage families. I have known of a variety of parsonage pets: dogs, cats, goldfish, turtles, chickens, assorted rodents, rabbits, horses, goats, snakes, spiders, one duck-billed platypus,[7] and birds of varying hues. (I'm not sure we can count as pets the deer, fox, and squirrels that some families feed. Although I am sure that Saint Francis—of blessed memory—would delight in these creatures, I doubt there is a parsonage anywhere that lends itself to housing deer, fox, and squirrels.)

And that comes to the heart of the matter: where do these pets live?[8] Another person might word the question: "Just where do you want to keep those fleas?" It can be dreadful. One pastor told of moving into a parsonage and discovering that his predecessor had determined that the hall closet made an ideal litter box for the cat. Another colleague described moving in behind the menagerie of seven cats and three dogs that graced the parsonage home before him.

Parsonage committees worry about long-term damage to a house (caused either by exuberant pets or indoor baseball games). These concerns are legitimate. Anyone who has tried to remove the smell of cat urine from a carpet can appreciate the apprehension. Anyone who has tried to extract dog hair from a living room couch can understand the trepidation. Anyone who has seen a dining room chair become a puppy's favorite chew toy can grasp the anxiety.

In the three preceding sentences, I have described the 1 percent of circumstances that make it difficult for the other 99 percent of parsonage families. Of course, responsible pet owners—in a parsonage or not—control their pets. (In over twenty-six years of having a dog inside the parsonage, our family has never had a single complaint or frown or disapproving glare—at least not related to the dog!) Some people do not like animals in a house. I respect that. Each time we left a parsonage, we paid for the services of cleaners and pest control visits, which assured our successors of inheriting a pet-free house. Of course, for our own sense of appropriateness, we maintained those levels of cleanliness and flea-free conditions throughout our years in each parsonage.

What are options if a congregation (probably because of previous bad experience) has a firm, unbending policy against pets in the parsonage? Here are some possibilities, some more desirable than others and some calling for a bit of pious negotiation: (1) Find a new home for the pet; (2) provide backyard facilities for the animal;[9] (3) agree on limited pet access within the house; (4) find someone who will keep the pet until you are living elsewhere; (5) keep the pet in a pen even if in the house;[10] (6) replace all flea-bearing critters with things that have fins; (7) train your pet to bite any visitors; (8) allow the animal(s) inside only at night or in cases of dangerous weather; (9) make a security deposit against damages; (10) sign a statement agreeing to leave parsonage as you found it (or better); (11) ask for a third-party intervention; (12) have the cat's claws deactivated;[11] (13) explain to your pet that you are leaving the ordained ministry because of fleas; (14) find a pet lover in the congregation who can help others in the congregation understand that pets do not destroy a house; (15) have a letter from your previous congregation indicating that your guinea pig actually improved the property value of the parsonage;[12] (16) offer to have a six-month trial period with your pet(s) in the parsonage; (17) point out that if the pet armadillo cannot come, your family will not come; (18) keep your pet cocker spaniel at the church, saying, "We have to keep Brownie at the church because you will not allow her to be at the parsonage"; (19) make sure that the "no pets" policy applies to the pet you have—bird in a cage, fish in a bowl, cricket in a cage, and so forth; (20) say no to the assignment;[13] (21) show the parsonage committee a picture of Jesus holding a baby lamb; (22) get the advice of your pastor-parish relations committee or pastoral advisory committee; (23) invite parsonage committee members to see the arrangements you have made for your pet at the parsonage; (24) be clear as to the source and rationale for the "no pets" policy; (25) have your ten-year-old daughter (tissues in hand) appeal to the recalcitrant committee; (26) at the peril of creating an unsealable fissure in church life, ignore the policy; (27) ask how most pet owners in the community handle their pets; (28) discuss what ought to be (and will be) off-limits for the pet; (29) explain your pet's previous history of behavior as a house pet; (30) offer to exchange your dog for a pet buffalo.

(DISCLAIMER: Dear Reader, please know that some of these

suggestions are made in jest. I do not recommend a buffalo as a house pet.[14] Once I got started, I wanted to get to thirty options. Mea culpa, mea culpa.)

And what, alas, when a pet dies? Frisky knew only one parsonage, so we buried him in the woods back of that house. Snoopy and Pommes Frites had moved with us, so we had them cremated and took their ashes with us to the next move. (OK, we had buried Snoopy's cremains, so we dug up some dirt more or less where we had buried the ashes.) A couple of questions: Does the parsonage family want to leave a deceased pet behind? Does the church object to a series of burials by a series of parsonage families? Goldfish and guinea pigs are easier to move to a final resting place. A buffalo would be another matter.

So much space has been devoted to the question of pets that one can sense that this can be a battleground for some parsonage families. Do not panic. Something can usually be worked out. Obviously, pastoral families will be impeccable in their care of both pet and parsonage. To fail to be good stewards of the parsonage by letting pets run amok is an invitation to have a breakdown in pastoral work. The parsonage household that abuses a parsonage (pets or otherwise) has made life much tougher for colleagues who follow. These are good touch points for making clear one's values in ministry, in relationships, and in discipleship.

As you prepare to move to a parsonage, make sure that the local church knows of any special family needs. Does the bathroom need to be wheelchair accessible? Is a safety rail needed in the shower? Many denominations have parsonage standards that seek to make these homes good and pleasant places for families in all kinds of circumstances.

Children growing up in parsonages are exposed to a range of the human condition. (They also learn early on that what they hear at home stays at home.) The opportunity to live in a variety of communities and to attend a mixture of schools and to have a diversity of friends can actually benefit the maturity and poise of a PK.[15] Far from being shielded from "the real world," parsonage children meet the world of the hungry, the impoverished, the broken, the lost, the suffering, as well as the world of the victorious, the proud, the recovered, the gracious, the saved, the empowered. That's not a bad thing!

Sometimes parsonage families discover what non-parsonage families discover: they can no longer helpfully live together. The visibility of the pastor and spouse and children makes this broken place particularly hard to bear. If separation or divorce begins to speak its word to the hearts of pastor and spouse, that voice needs to be shared with trusted supervisors. What is the best way to prevent this disturbed place in the parsonage home from becoming a divisive spirit in the congregation? It certainly helps if all parties are on the same sheet of music as to what is happening.

Single pastors (with or without children) may encounter situations in which they are expected to make do with less in the parsonage because they are single. Alas. The parsonage should be a home for single pastors as much as for married pastors. The same need for space, privacy, household furnishings, pet policy, and the like are present for the single pastor too!

Maybe I am spoiled. I grew up in parsonages and lived to tell about it. Our son grew up in parsonages; and he is a sensitive, mature, contributing Christian layperson. There can be stresses on family fabric in parsonages, but the weave can also produce beauty and strength and joy.

CHAPTER 5

THE TOILET SEAT DOESN'T WORK

She seemed like such a lovely, sweet person. I did not perceive her to be conniving or manipulative. My wife, Toni, and I were enjoying lunch with her, along with her husband and another clergy colleague. The seafood restaurant in the coastal city was inviting for all kinds of fun and casual conversation.

Then she said: "Let me tell you about the toilet seat." It was not the topic I had expected as our flounder plates and shrimp salads were being delivered. "It would not work," she said, "and I could not get the parsonage committee to do a thing about it." I gave my most sympathetic grunt.

"I got my chance," she went on, "when there was a small meeting of church officers at the parsonage. I served lots of iced tea. *Lots* of tea." An image began to form in my mind.

"When finally the chair of the church council asked me if he could use the bathroom, I gladly consented, making sure he was directed to the one with the broken toilet seat. That seat was a terrible thing for my husband." She tried to be helpfully descriptive: "The seat would not stay upright when it was lifted," she explained. "It would fall back at the most inopportune times." The image in my mind became clearer.

"Well," she finished, "the church council chair went into bathroom and when he came out he said simply, 'Karen,[1] will it be all right if I have someone come by tomorrow and fix that toilet? It doesn't seem to be working right.'"

Not bad for a lovely, sweet, non-conniving, non-manipulative woman!

Even the best of houses is not likely to be free of problems from time to time. In a parsonage, however, the issue can be kicked up a notch unless everyone is clear on how to proceed when repairs need action, furniture needs replacing, and painting needs doing.

One of the best systems I encountered was a decision to grant the pastoral family $300 each year to spend as it chose for the parsonage. Get a better lawnmower? Buy a new chair for the study? Get a magazine rack for the den? These purchases were still parsonage property, but it gave some freedom of input to the parsonage family circle. To be sure, there were times of unfortunate decisions, but on balance the method worked well.

Some churches have determined a system of getting repairs done by indicating that the family arranges for the work and sends the bill to the church. Some finance committees feel more secure in that arrangement if the understanding is that no repairs in excess of X number of dollars be made without some further approval. An alternative plan is to have a pre-approved list of repair personnel who are on call for the church and parsonage.[2]

A good approach, actually required in some denominational polity, is to have regular, planned visits by the parsonage committee or trustees. They can see for themselves what needs doing and can better understand what provisions would make a better house for the pastor's home. There are two sides to such a visit: (1) Does the parsonage family have what it needs? (2) Is the church keeping up the maintenance on this property it owns? Truth to tell, it is hard for this joint "look-see" to feel like anything other than "show and tell" time for the pastor and household. The parsonage family will benefit from understanding these checkups as being in their own interest. It can set to rest rumors that the parsonage is getting beat up; it can alert the congregation to unanticipated housing issues; it can help all concerned see the parsonage as a joint venture: their house, my home. Unannounced visits, no matter how well meaning, are unfair.

Parsonages compete with other good causes for the budget dollar. Missions? Sunday school? Evangelism? Salaries? Church building repairs? Local benevolences? Church library?[3] Keyboard purchase? Parking lot improvement? DISCIPLE Bible study? Nursery furniture? Which of these items do you want to step aside so money can be spent on the parsonage? (Can you say "guilt"?)

The answer, certainly, is none of the above. The parsonage takes its place along with the other vital ministries of the congregation. The parsonage is for the benefit of the church's ministry (it's not a bonus for the pastor) and should be lifted up as yet another way the congregation makes possible the ministry of Jesus Christ.

Sadly, sometimes the parsonage loses all the financial battles. (The parsonage, like any other ministry, must take its lumps occasionally for other causes. The goal is not to have the showplace of the community; the goal is to provide such housing that the pastor is free to be the leader, coach, pastor, prophet, and priest that she or he needs to be.)

One clergy colleague portrayed one parsonage as having, shall we say, unfulfilled promise. He wrote: "It was a night with heavy rain pounding with rhythm the roof of the parsonage; it made for peaceful sleeping. As morning dawned and the coffee was brewing, I went to the basement where our family had turned a corner of the crypt into a den, fully equipped with sofa, end table, and television. When I stepped on the freshly painted floor of the basement (that painting was a summer project completed by my daughter and me), something crept onto my ankles, something wet and cold. Visions of various forms of animal life flashed through my head. I turned on the light and discovered that the floor was flooded from that evening's rain.

"From corner to corner, I could see that there was a new wading pool waiting to be cleaned up. My wife and daughter heard me (husband, father, pastor) express myself in terms that drew on my Anglo-Saxon heritage and that presented evidence of my misspent youth. I called the chairperson of the church trustees and he indicated that the basement had a problem with leaking. (Uh, at this point, this was not news to me.)

"He said he thought it had been taken care of and wished me well in draining the 'pool'. The problem was that there was no drain. There was no way to get the water out of the basement but with a combination of mop, bucket, and shop vac. Each pail of water collected had to be hauled up a *fight*[4] of stairs, then through the kitchen, and into the backyard.

"Each time I made that trip, I was reminded of someone telling me that something she learned from the Noah's ark story was this: 'If you can't fight or flee, float!' So, I floated that day and all the days thereafter when the rain found its way to the parsonage basement. I was not successful in getting the church to fix the problem during my stay there. The parsonage committee asked me to attend its meeting with my successor. I asked him if he had a life jacket and raft for this new journey. Some were more amused by this insight than others.

"Today, after a hard rain, my wife and I still look at each other with a question in our minds: 'Do you suppose . . . ?' God bless all parsonage families everywhere with rain in their lives!"

I am confident that this pastor went about getting this leak fixed in all the right ways, through all the correct channels. But nothing was done. Did the congregation not care about the damage being done to its property? Was there no appreciation of the waste of the pastor's time and energy in emptying the water? Were they trying to establish the basement as the site of future baptismal immersions? What was going on in this situation?

I have the advantage of having no idea, so I can pontificate on the subject with great authority. My hunch is that everyone thought it was someone else's job to take care of it. Church trustees? Parsonage committee? Pastoral advisory committee? Pastor? Chair of church council? Captain of the softball team? Most people do not want to step deliberately into someone else's territory or to imply that someone else is not doing his or her job, so voilá! Nothing happens.

It would be helpful if church leadership sat down and mapped out a scheme of contacts for parsonage concerns. Whom does the pastor contact if the furnace goes out at 2:00 A.M. on February 15? Whom does the pastor contact if the drapes in the living room are bleached out by the sun? Whom does the pastor contact if the well water seems too full of iron? Whom does the pastor contact if the antique chair in the dining room breaks in normal usage? Whom does the pastor contact if the antique chair in the dining room breaks because Child No. 1 threw it at Child No. 2? Whom does the pastor contact if the broadband computer service goes down? Whom does the pastor contact if there is a leak in the roof (or, for that matter, in the basement!)? Whom does the pastor contact if the hot water heater goes out? Whom does the pastor call if there is a mold or mildew problem? Whom does the pastor call if a hurricane drops trees and limbs into the parsonage yard? Whom does the pastor call if there is evidence of termites? Whom does the pastor call if her child's baseball breaks a window?

As you can see, the list is without limit. No wonder it gets confusing, and no wonder that work falls through the cracks. One system is to have a single contact who would "farm out" the problem as appropriate. A person in such a role needs to be organized and have a good sense of follow-through. The semi-annual (or annual) walk-through of the parsonage provides a chance to reflect on how the system is working.

Why can't the pastor take care of most of these things himself or herself? Probably can. If the house belonged to the pastor, the next step would usually be clear. It is this matter of living in a house belonging to someone else. (Renters can have the same problem.) Few pastors would expect the church to change light bulbs for them, but what about painting a bedroom? Who chooses the color?[5] Few pastors would expect the church to plant flowers by the front door, but what about planting a vegetable garden where the parsonage has lawn? Few pastors would expect the church to select his or her books, but who decides about building a new bookcase for the study?

If relations are open between congregation and pastor, most of these issues are handled with casual conversation. Formal checks and balances may be needed in the early days of a pastoral relationship or in situations in which there is already tension in the pastor-church rapport.

What makes "their house" into "my home"? Having your own things to enjoy and to stir memories and to establish your own identity as a family are parts of that process. Some congregations and denominational judicatories have begun policies of not furnishing the entire parsonage. That works well when the congregation understands that it helps a family to put its personal stamp on this house.

And when it does not work well? Consider this account. A pastor tells of moving to a new appointment, pleased that the church has invested more than $30,000 in getting the parsonage "right" before the new family arrived. Women of the church with decorating skills poured their best judgment into the work. Colors were coordinated. Pictures were put up that matched wall colors and furniture styles. Elegant.

When the parsonage family arrived, there was no place to put anything of their own. The parsonage committee provided a list of rules: no moving furniture without permission; no pets; no new holes in the walls. The family was advised that the homemade kitchen shelf crafted by the wife's father was "too country" to put up.

A favorite of the family was a painting showing an old-timey man and woman holding hands. The caption read: "Caldwells, established March 7, 1983,"[6] the couple's wedding date. This piece had been a wedding gift, and the Caldwells had always used it at the front door to greet and welcome visitors. At their new home, they put the painting on a waiting nail.

The doorbell rang. One of the decorating team from the church held in her hand the offending item, the Caldwell's painting. "This is not appropriate for the outside of the house," she said.

As she continued her visit, the woman from the Good Taste Police marveled at how beautiful the parsonage was now. "In fact," the visitor added, "after visiting this lovely place, I'll go now and look at my house and want to throw up!"

The vexed pastor's wife said, "Well, at least you have your own house in which to throw up!"

This horror story represents good purposes gone awry. Everyone wanted things to be right. The church wanted the new pastor to find (and be pleased with) all the resources and beauty that had gone into getting things ready. Those who made the decorating choices wanted nothing but the best for their pastor. It is hard to fault a parsonage committee for that. But it is hard to let go of one's own investment (emotional, financial, aesthetic) in such a project. Could some of the decisions be delayed until the new family could be part of it? Could some of the arrangements be left undone so the parsonage flock could incorporate their personal things? Could the newcomers be kept apprised of the plans so they would not be surprised and without input? Could the clergy family live with the existing parsonage long enough to develop some relationship context for making the changes?[7]

The stories of how parsonage families get abused by misdirected parsonage committees are more fun to tell than the accounts of responsive, helpful church members. Truth to tell, we clergy remember the accounts of dismay and disaster precisely because they are unusual. Most of the time, the leak gets repaired, the family pictures get hung, the chair gets replaced, the wall gets painted, and the toilet seat gets fixed. And we are grateful.

Chapter 6

Guess Who's Coming to Supper (and Breakfast and Lunch)

A congregation provides a parsonage for its pastor and the pastor's family. The parsonage is the pastor's home. So far, can we agree?

Is there a problem if the mother-in-law comes to live with the family? (Probably not.)

Is there a problem if an exchange student comes to live at the parsonage? (Probably not.)

Is there an expectation that the parsonage will house members of touring choirs and visiting preachers? (Maybe so.)

Is there an expectation that the pastor will not sublease part of the parsonage to make a little spending money? (Almost certainly.)

Is there likely to be discontent if the pastor frequently invites homeless people to share the shelter of a parsonage room? (Oh, yeah!)

Does anyone care if the pastor's college roommate comes for a weekend visit? (Surely not.)

How will people feel about Cousin Carl bringing his malamute to stay at the parsonage when Carl comes for the family reunion? (See above in chapter 4 on "pets.")

Who gets to stay in the parsonage if pastor and spouse go into legal separation? (Tougher question than you might think.)

What will be the attitude of the congregation if the pastor's hobby is repairing junk cars on the front lawn of the parsonage? (Gasp and sputter.)

Who will care if the pastor invites prisoners on work release to stay at the parsonage? (Is Jesus smiling?)

Who cares if a single pastor has an overnight guest? (Lots of people with just one question: What gender?)

Is there likely to be concern if the parsonage teenager has a sleepover at the parsonage? (Probably only from those trying to sleep in the house.)

Some of these questions would be non-issues if the pastor owned the house. The issues surface because the pastor's home is in a building owned by someone else. It has been said, "The right of your fist ends just short of my nose." Where does the pastor's right end to have a parsonage home to his or her own choosing?

One way to approach that question is to appreciate that communication is the key. If there is any doubt about there being a mutual understanding, open the doors of conversation! The arrogance of "this is mine and you can't do anything about it" (from the point of view of either pastor or church) is going to damage ministry offered in the name of Jesus Christ. The parsonage is not the pastor's to use in any way the pastor chooses; it is the pastor's to use in any way that advances the witness to our Lord. The parsonage is not the church's to control in any way the congregation chooses; it is the church's to control in any way that advances the witness to our Lord.

When there is disagreement about the pastor's use versus the church's control, no one benefits from a surprise attack.

Think on these things:

Item: "My cousin's house burned down last week, so she and her two children need a place to stay. We are thinking about inviting them to stay with us at the parsonage for the next six weeks."

Item: "Preacher, some of us who drive by your house on the way to work have noticed somebody's car parked there each morning, but gone during the day. There's nothing going on we need to know about, is there?"

Item: "We are excited that Hans Beecher is going to be living with us for this semester. He is an exchange student from Germany and will be in the eleventh grade just like our son Derek."

Item: "I'm renting the spare bedroom at the parsonage to a student at the university. She needed a safe place to study, and we needed the income. Sounds like a deal, right?"

Item: "No one in our family smokes, but one of the men from the shelter has been staying with us at the parsonage and he smokes. You might need to replace the drapes in the den; I think the smoke has gotten into them."

Item: "Reverend Lynn, we know that you are sort of into environmental things and don't like to use the clothes dryer, but some of us think you should not have things hanging on that outdoor clothesline on Sunday."[1]

Item: "I did not like that big TV antenna on top of the parsonage, so I got it taken down and had cable installed. The church should get the bill."

POP QUIZ! Question 1: Read back over these items and imagine what might be the next words spoken.[2] Question 2: Were the statements made in each item the healthiest and most helpful ways to deal with the issue? Question 3: What is another way this topic might have been addressed? Question 4: How could the matter be discussed so there are all winners and no losers? Question 5: How does a pastor determine when something is worth "going to the mat" for?[3] Question 6: How does one handle life's conflicts between good values and good values?[4]

END OF POP QUIZ. How did you do?

More than one pastor has heard a knock on the door late at night and met there a parishioner trying to get away from an abusive situation. The parsonage is seen by some as an extension of the church, a safe place providing sanctuary for those who need a place of escape or hiding. (I do not know that law enforcement personnel see the parsonage as sanctuary in quite the same way that some traditions see the church building.)

Pastor X[5] shared with me this incident from his early parsonage living. One of his nearby neighbors was a church member, but her husband, Glenn,[6] had never quite "gotten religion." Glenn had developed a rather well-earned reputation for drinking too much and thus creating opportunities for pastoral intervention. A former pastor had advised Pastor X to move gently if called upon to handle Glenn while Glenn was intoxicated.

The parsonage doorbell rang late one night. It rang again and then again, with obvious urgency. It sounded like trouble. The pastor's wife and two sons were in the living room as the door opened, revealing the very distraught neighbor, pounding on the storm door, pleading, "Preacher! Preacher! You have got to let me in! Glenn is drunk again and he says he is going to kill me! Please, can I come in?" The storm door gave way to the woman's insistent tugging, opened up, and the woman thrust herself into the living room.

Pastor X talked with this unexpected guest, who did not calm down until the pastor had locked the storm door, double-locked the front door, and secured the safety chain as well.

"Do you really think he'd kill you if he found you?"

"Yes! When he is like this, I think he could do that!"

"Does he have a gun?"

"No, but he has a pitchfork!"

As the woman said this, headlights begin to shine through the parsonage's big picture window. The vehicle idled next to the front porch and stopped. No other truck in the community sounded like Glenn's 1968 V-8 Chevy with four-wheel drive and dual exhausts. It was the loudest truck around, and everyone recognized it.

The pastor watched as Glenn walked unsteadily toward the steps and sat down. What followed was a strange pastoral conversation, conducted with both men bellowing at the top of their lungs back and forth through locked storm door and locked front door. It did not sound like Rogerian therapy.[7]

"Preacher, I know she's in there! I don't mean no harm to you, but you better let her out now!"

"I cannot let her out if you are going to hurt her. And you cannot come in. My wife and children are in here. Now you go home and settle a bit."

"I'm settled right where I want to be!"

"Now you go on home. I will call the sheriff's office and they will send somebody here so you can talk with your wife with the deputy present."

"I said for you to open that door! I have come here to kill her!"

"How are you going to do that?"

"With a pitchfork."

"Where is it?"

"I got it right here beside the porch. Let her out!"

In response to the call from the pastor's wife, a sheriff's patrol car passed slowly in front of the parsonage. Glenn watched the deputy go by. Glenn got up and walked slowly to his truck, put the pitchfork gently into the back of the truck, got into his truck, backed carefully out of the driveway, and headed in the direction of his home.

Glenn's wife refused the pastor's advice to file a complaint against her husband. And twenty-five years later, Pastor X has learned that Glenn and his wife still live together.

At one level, there might seem to be a strange humor in a man standing with a pitchfork as a weapon, but at the heart of this report is a tragic story of inexcusable abuse. What has Glenn's wife lived with for all these years? Why has no helpful intervention occurred? What gifts have been lost to the world because of Glenn's alcoholic rage and because of his wife's having to live in a cage created by that rage?

In the context of this chapter, another subject grows out of this report: How does a parsonage serve as a safe house?

It should be safe for the parsonage family. Of course.

Should it be a safe place for persons in trouble? Yes, but would we not also hope that would be true for any Christian home?

What makes the parsonage different is what makes a pastor different who wears a clerical collar.[8] If someone on the street spots a person wearing a clerical collar, the passerby assumes some things about the wearer: this person will help me if I need help; this person will listen to me if I want to talk; this person represents love and justice. (Distressingly, news of recent years has made the person in the clerical collar also a little suspect.) If a house is known to be a parsonage, it is like putting a giant clerical collar around it. Those who see it make assumptions about what they will find within: hospitality, care, support.

Sometimes the cover belies what is in a book, and sometimes the collar does not reflect the person wearing it and sometimes a parsonage does not contain the spirit signaled by its presence. Nevertheless, the very fact that a particular house is a parsonage suggests to visitors what they might find behind the door.

There is something else that happens when a pastor wears a clerical collar. That pastor knows that he or she is being seen by the world as a representative of the church and of the Lord of the church. Do pastors behave differently when they are aware that those who see them know them as representatives of Christ? Some clergy think that the collar is a sign to the world that she or he is ready to serve. Is the parsonage also such a sign? Is life in and from the parsonage lived in awareness that "this place represents the availability of Jesus Christ in this community"?

Clerical collars are worn willingly. Parsonages might not "wear" clerical collars willingly. Maybe that reality generates resentment within the parsonage family. "I did not choose to live here, and I did not choose to have to be professionally Christian all the time!" is the way one spouse put it. Folks, it goes with the territory. Families in a parsonage do not live in an anonymous house.[9] As such, what goes on in the parsonage reflects positively or negatively on the witness of the church. We might wish it were not so, but that's the way life is put together.

In the King James Version of 1 Thessalonians 5:22, we get this caution: "Abstain from all appearance of evil." The appearance, the perception of evil can be as spoiling for a ministry as the reality of wrongdoing. Even when generous heart and pure intent motivate the parsonage household, the public perception of evil does damage. (The unmarried pastor may sleep five rooms removed from a guest of the opposite sex, but to do so is to risk one's ministry for something that never even happened!)

Some of this chapter hints of potential conflict between the "rights" of the parsonage family (to have whomever it chooses as guests, for example) and the "rights" of the congregation to make decisions about property it owns (no pets allowed, for example). Christian dialogue should not center on rights. All of life is gift. Those who are called into a set-apart ministry are called not to rights, but to a yoke. When a yoke is put upon oxen, it is not so the owner can beat and abuse the oxen. (So there is no place for taking advantage of clergy and abusing their humanity.) However, when a yoke is put on oxen, it is so the beasts can more faithfully be obedient to the will of the driver.

Let's stretch that image just a little more. The best work done by oxen is done when two are yoked together, to serve together, to toil together, both trying to cooperate to do the will of the master. Let's rejoice when the congregation's parsonage and the pastor's parsonage are yoked in service together for Jesus Christ!

CHAPTER 7

WHEN IS A GNU NEW?

O K. I could not resist. A gnu (sometimes called a wildebeest, but that is another story) is a type of antelope. It lives in a state of constant movement. It can travel hundreds of miles. It moves on, always hoping the grass will be greener in the next plain. Of course, occasionally a gnu gets eaten up by a hungry lion. Does that sound like any pastors you know?

Clergy, unlike gnus, do not always have to move in order to find a better place in which to live. Sometimes, a pastor has the chance to be around when a new parsonage is to be built.[1] It is fun and frightening. It is challenging and comforting. It is frustrating and fulfilling. It is cooperative and conflictive. Do you get the picture? Being part of the construction of a new parsonage touches every possible emotion and pushes every possible button in the congregation.

In some ways, it is easier for a pastor to help get a church built than it is to help get a parsonage constructed. Many parishioners do not feel they have major expertise when it comes to designing and building a church. But most folks have great confidence about what is needed in a house. This confidence translates into multiple opinions about size, shape, materials, number of bathrooms, location, contractor, lighting fixtures, furnishings, fences, size of bedrooms, handicap accessibility, carpets (or hardwood), what to keep from the old house and what not to carry to the new site, whether to have room for a garden, window treatments, spot for washing machine, necessity of toothpick holder, and just how many bookshelves are needed. You get the picture. (Well, you may not get the picture; someone else might be choosing the pictures for the wall!)

Congregations in some denominations have guidelines to follow when building a parsonage.[2] These procedures seek to establish sound financial footing, work to assure accessible facilities, and try to create a common standard. Behind this practice of common denominational policy is an awareness that pastors should be assigned or called on the basis of congregational mission and pastoral gifts, not on whether the pastor has enough closet space.[3]

In deciding to build (or purchase) a parsonage, church membership often begins with a basic question: Should the parsonage match the kind of housing lived in by most of the congregation? In answering that question, decision-makers need to keep in mind that the purpose of the parsonage system is to facilitate ministry in the name of Jesus Christ. "Excess" in a parsonage does not signal a spirit of Christian servanthood. "Scarcity" in a parsonage does not signal that this is the work of a monarch, not of a beggar. It is valuable in a pastorate for the clergy to identify with the congregation. Neither a house that widely exceeds congregational experience nor one that greatly understates congregational experience will foster a healthy pastor-parish relationship. The parsonage is the pastor's home. What kind of home will allow the best ministry to occur?

When designing or selecting a new parsonage, a congregation would do well to talk with those with the most parsonage experience: clergy families. Pastoral households have often lived in several different parsonages and have good notions of what works and what does not work. Although the views of the current parsonage family are important, decisions should be made beyond the personal tastes and preferences of that one family. There are ways of making opportunities available for personal expressions without locking future families into an unsuitable time warp.[4]

Although basic matters (zoning, building regulations and permits, good quality construction, safety, flexible design, financial appropriateness, TV hook-up, Internet access) apply to any house being built, there are some issues that are more or less distinctive to a parsonage. Here are some questions that might be asked about a new parsonage.[5] (1) Is there a good location for storing moving boxes? (2) Can there be a place for entertaining without intruding on family personal space? (3) Is there room for an in-house study? (4) What provision is made for the pastor's large storehouse of books? (5) Is there storage space for the family's personal items that "don't fit" this particular parsonage?[6] (6) Is the security such that the family feels safe late at night? (7) If there are "public" spaces in the house—for church meetings, for example—are these areas clearly separate from the family's "home space"? (8) Is the location reasonably accessible to hospitals and other places the pastor might need to visit regularly (and sometimes at odd hours)? (9) If the pastor's main study is at the parsonage, does the study have a private entrance for visitors? (10) Does the house sit on a wooded mountain lot overlooking a placid lake with soft breezes blowing?[7] (11) Is there a first-floor bedroom? (12) Are all necessary areas of the house accessible to persons with mobility limitation? (13) Will signage identify the house as a parsonage? (14) Have appropriate denominational officials been consulted?[8] (15) Is there a place for the pastor's pet giraffe? (16) Have decisions been made as to who will have keys to the house? (17) Is there a utility space available that could be used in a variety of ways, depending on the parsonage family's needs (extra bedroom, storage, hobby room, indoor eggplant farm, spouse's office, playroom, media room, and so forth?)[9] (18) What is the advice of the current parsonage family?

Although the renovation of a parsonage is not quite the same as building from scratch, such a project has its own set of concerns. Where will the parsonage family stay while the work is being done? (Rented house? Friendly members? In a small corner of the parsonage? Extended vacation? Motel? SUV? Public streets? Trip to the Holy Lands? Sunday school classroom? The options seem endless!)

It is difficult to coordinate parsonage renovations when the departing pastor leaves on the same day as the incoming pastor shows up. (In some areas, the tradition is "Old out by noon; new in by 1:00." That doesn't leave much time for scrambling workers!) One pastor describes arriving at dusk on moving day. Every light in the parsonage was blazing. Ladders and workers were everywhere "like ants on a discarded apple." It seems that the new parsonage family had noticed the paint-deprived condition of the house on a pre-move visit, so now church members were frantically trying to get the place in order: painting, repair work, and cleaning sent volunteers in multiple directions. It was organized chaos (or perhaps chaotic organization). The pastor slipped into the bathroom, more or less out of necessity. He was astonished to see a fully clothed man sitting in the bathtub. In the man's right hand was a hammer. In his left hand was a chisel. The man looked up and said, "Welcome, preacher," as if that explained everything. Saying nothing else, the man in the tub began to chip away at something on the tub. Knowing that dialogue is important in establishing pastoral relationships, the new pastor asked, "And what are we doing here, my friend?" Without missing a beat, the worker replied, "Iron." "Oh?" the pastor offered, continuing his best, mystified effort to connect. "Yep," the man replied.[10]

By now the pastor's curiosity exceeded his need for privacy in the bathroom, so he pushed ahead: "Iron? How so?" The king of the tub answered, "Iron. In the water. Stains. Porcelain. Nothing works on it." Chisel in hand, he resumed, "I'm just trying to chip away the stain." (Alternative: In the back of my phone book, there is an advertising section called "Bathtubs and Sinks.")

When should a congregation fix up the present parsonage instead of building or buying a different house? One way to consider that issue is to test the existing parsonage against the eighteen questions listed above. Intangible values are not to be ignored: tradition, present visibility, missional focus, financial priorities. The bottom-line question shows up again: Which direction is going to be the most positive for the witness to Jesus Christ?

Although cosmetic changes can make a place more livable, renovation often means exploring structural changes and hidden repairs. Feeding God's creatures is a Christian virtue, but that vital act of piety has to be balanced against a concern that providing meals for termites might be beyond the mission of a congregation![11] Fixing damage to joints and joists is more valuable for a house than repainting the dining room, but often it is of less interest to those who are paying the bills.

Hurricanes and tornadoes and winds of varying sorts can drop trees (and automobiles) on top of parsonage roofs. This is an emergency. If the response plan in place does not work, perhaps the pastor might consider the philosophy of "It's easier to get forgiveness than it is to get permission." Get the immediate problem fixed! The failure of a congregation to act in such an emergency (like a hurricane) often happens because the entire community is traumatized by the storm. The pastor is going to be under stress and emotional strain as she moves among the shocked and hurting people; at the same time, the parsonage family needs physical and emotional support. Congregations in connectional structures understand that there are other congregations in the connection who will be coming to help. Congregations not part of a connectional system might well identify brother/sister congregations in other places with a mutual pact of coming to help when there are emergency circumstances.[12]

Even when work is done by volunteers, it is important to have qualified professional supervision. An architect can guide a congregation away from costly mistakes in design. A contractor can direct a congregation toward alternative solutions. A realtor can broaden the reach of a search. Unless these persons donate their services, these involvements cost money. A congregation may feel it is having to decide, for example, between adding a nice garage to the project or having an architect. Such a choice needs to be made with a long-range view in mind: which of these valuable assets is needed now, and which of these valuable assets could come later?

It is a sacred responsibility to house God's children (Matthew 25:31-46).[13] It is a serious matter. A pastor ought not to be frivolous in making demands upon a congregation; a congregation ought not to be parsimonious in meeting the needs of the parsonage family. After all, we are on the same team!

CHAPTER 8

VIEW FROM THE PEW

Reverend Lopez, it must be nice not to have to pay taxes."
"Ms. Burke, how does it feel to have everything provided for you?"
"Mr. Ayers, I wish somebody paid all of my bills."
"Esther, dear, I know you won't mind if we have the mission study group meet with you at the parsonage."
"Pastor, what expenses do you have other than food?"
These misconceptions about parsonage life are balanced with the multitude of laypeople who understand that (a) clergy pay taxes, (b) everything is not provided, (c) no one else pays the pastor's bills, (d) meetings at the parsonage should be by pastoral family invitation, and (e) parsonage families have to spend money too!

Although a few parishioners think of the parsonage as a gift to the pastor, most recognize that such housing is for the convenience of the congregation. The pastor gets no equity and may have little choice in the details of his or her living space. (On the other hand, the pastor has no risk of financial investment in the house and its upkeep.)

Some congregations want to get out of the parsonage "business" and give a housing allowance to the pastor. Such an approach removes one financial risk from the church. It also allows the possibility of the pastoral family being more content with its housing. Housing allowances reduce the hassle of maintenance from church members. This arrangement works easiest in denominations with congregational polity; housing allowances put stress on systems in which pastors are assigned their places of service. ("Can we appoint Helen Zachary to that church? Can she afford a down payment?") A congregation with a housing allowance might make it difficult for some pastors to be appointed to its mission. There could be a shortage of desirable housing; the pastor might prefer housing well out of the community's area; the pastor might not be in a financial position to purchase and maintain housing; rental property might be unavailable.

Of course, numerous pastors prefer a parsonage over a housing allowance.[1] Why? (1) Having a parsonage provided makes one less matter of decision and stress at the times of frequent moves. (2) They had rather make their real estate investment in a potential retirement home. (3) They had rather make their real estate investment in a vacation home. (4) Low pastoral income may not allow purchase of good housing. (5) The quickness with which some pastoral changes are made does not give adequate time for careful choice about a house. (6) The church community might be one in which the pastor would not choose to make a housing investment. (7) They prefer not to be engaged in risky real estate buying and selling as they move from one pastorate to another to another. (8) Second-career pastors might already own a house and do not want two mortgages. (9) In some systems, pastors might be caught having to move from parsonage to housing allowance to parsonage, back and forth, as various congregations had varying approaches to housing arrangements. (10) They have aligned themselves with a polity in which pastoral assignments (and thus locale) are made by persons other than the pastor and congregation. (United Methodists: read this as bishop and cabinet.)[2]

Occasionally, a congregation that has provided a housing allowance for its pastor receives a pastor who wants (or needs) a parsonage. The transition back to parsonage does not necessarily entail purchase of a house; the church might opt to rent a house for the pastor. This frees the pastor from having to seek and find housing; it frees the church from the kind of maintenance that would fall to the owner of the property. Renting, rather than buying, a parsonage also gives flexibility for house size and locale, as various parsonage families bring differing needs.

But these pages are chiefly about life in a parsonage. How do members of a congregation view the parsonage? Home for the pastor? Our investment? Our gift to the pastor? Our maintenance problem? A base for ministry? A way to support our pastor? A way to free our pastor for her ministry? A way to be part of a connection of churches? Perhaps a pastoral advisory committee (pastor-parish relations committee) could see part of its duty to interpret the parsonage to the congregation.[3]

Faye Cardinal[4] was pastor of a group of churches who owned a parsonage together.[5] Wanting to spruce up the parsonage landscaping, one of the members decided to plant a tree in the front yard. He did not check with anyone at the churches and neglected to tell the Reverend Ms. Cardinal that he was going to show up with a tree in tow. He drove his tractor onto the parsonage yard and began using an auger to dig a hole for the tree. The noise of the machinery brought Faye Cardinal into her yard (she did live there, after all!) to face the sight of this gentleman, his eighty-year-old frame bouncing on top of the tractor seat.

Her surprise turned to shock when the man dismounted the tractor to try to adjust the auger. He bent over the tool, and its spinning screw caught his pants leg. The power of the turning auger ripped the pants from this would-be helper. He was obviously in trouble, so Faye ran to the tractor, ready to turn off its power. Alas, her city background gave her little knowledge of tractor switches and gears and keys, so she blundered among the options without success.

By now, the auger had completed its churning through the octogenarian's apparel, leaving him more or less as the Lord had delivered him some eighty years ago. Now free of the auger, he stepped to the tractor and cut off the power. That left the rather discomfited relationship of Pastor Cardinal and her newly disrobed parishioner.

She retreated to her car and grabbed a towel and her cell phone. The towel put to its obvious best use (given the circumstances), Faye turned her attention to calling the wife of the helper. Unabashed, as if this sort of thing happened regularly, the dutiful spouse drove over in the family car and picked up her ill-clad husband. The tree remained unplanted.

This account reveals one "view from the pew" about parsonages. Sometimes, individual members take parsonage ownership as a very personal matter and assume managerial and decorative responsibilities on their own. Of course, this is a boon when Mr. Hawkins fixes the hole in the fence without being asked or when Ms. Edwards repairs the doorbell she noticed broken on her most recent visit. The potential downside, however, is dual: (a) what should be corporate decisions get made individually, and (b) the parsonage household might well be left entirely out of the loop. At a minimum, such "helpers" need to call the parsonage and advise them of impending "helpfulness," and at best, such support should be channeled through the designated avenues determined by the parsonage committee or trustees or other responsible group.[6]

Some parishioners see the parsonage as a financial bonus for the pastor. ("I'd like not to have to pay rent." "I wish I didn't have a mortgage.") Although the parsonage is not part of clergy compensation, it does relieve the pastor of some real estate investment risk. The other side of that coin is that the pastor is often paid less because housing is provided; the pastor thus has no way to build equity in a house. Retirement years can be lean after a lifetime of parsonages.

There is a tension (surprise!) in weighing the privacy of a pastor's home against the congregation's desire to provide the best possible parsonage. When a congregation views the parsonage as "off limits" ("That's the pastor's home"), there can be a tendency for the clergy family to feel abandoned or ignored. When a congregation stays on top of parsonage matters ("Let's get a new sofa for the living room"), there can be a proclivity in the pastor's household to feel invaded and subordinate.

Parsonage families cannot expect full care and maintenance of the parsonage by the congregation if appropriate persons from the congregation never have access to the house. How can they fix what they don't know about? Some polities require such visits, but the way is smoother for fruitful conversation if the pastor's family schedules and invites such "tours."

Here is an account of one such arrangement (shared by the wife of a pastor): "Before we moved there, the church folks had not been in the parsonage for a long time. They did not realize that so much needed to be fixed. When they brought food on moving day, the committee looked around, consulted with the trustees, and said, 'Let's get started!' The work took three months. They offered to put us in a motel, but we stayed at the parsonage to do our part by helping them save that money. They were grateful and did even more to make improvements. Here we discovered that patience pays off and that when you pitch in to help, people are more than willing to do what needs to be done. When they finished, the parsonage was beautiful and we enjoyed our stay there so much!"

Several ingredients contributed to this happy ending: (1) The parsonage family let the church committee see things for themselves. (2) The committee responded immediately with a plan. (3) The plan was approved by the appropriate church decision-making groups. (4) The pastor's family cooperated with the plan and bore part of the stress of the work. (5) The parsonage household saw themselves as part of the effort to be good stewards of church funds. (6) Patience. (7) Patience. (8) Patience. (9) The congregation appreciated the "we're in this together" spirit of the pastoral family. (10) Patience. (11) Patience. (12) Recognize, celebrate, and enjoy![7]

It does get a bit confusing for the church community when Pastor C has a different view of parsonage life than did Pastor B, who felt differently about the matter than did Pastor A. As noted earlier in this book, it helps if these discussions can take place before moving day! Neither pastor nor church should assume they know how the other approaches parsonage questions. Ask! Share! Although an occasional antagonist will seek to undermine the mutual understandings and relationships, most pastors and most congregations really do want things to work well!

For some congregations, the expense and bother of providing a parsonage is just part of the "cost of doing business." Parsonage decisions come and go without making much impact on the spiritual journey of most of the people in the pews.[8] As a general rule, the larger the congregation, the less likely it is that Average Joe and Average Jill know much more than "I think the preacher lives in a parsonage." In mega-congregations, few know (and even fewer care) where the lead pastor lives. In churches of small membership, the relationships are often cozier, the secrets are fewer, and the involvement is higher. If 10 percent of the membership of a church is on the board of trustees or a parsonage committee,[9] it is likely that almost everyone in the congregation is going to know about the leaky faucet, the fleas in the kitchen, and the uncut grass in the front yard. The view (of the parsonage) from the pew is going to be more sharply focused in a church with fewer than 100 in attendance than it is in a church with 1,000 in attendance. Naturally, if the parsonage is next door to the other church facilities, people will notice the yin/yang of parsonage existence more quickly than if the parsonage is a couple of miles away!

Congregational views of the parsonage, and parsonage views of the congregation, are helped when everyone remembers that all life journeys have not been the same, but that God has been present in each with grace, seeking a place in that journey. What might appear to be a deliberate snub or intentional act of defiance might simply be a difference in the view from the path on which each has been walking. One recent seminary graduate was taking his first rural appointment. After an exploration of his new parsonage home, he thought his "tour guide" from the church was a bit rude in pointing to a small building (4 x 4 x 4 feet) in the backyard. "See that building, Preacher? You check that light every day and make sure it is on!" Those seemed like abrupt instructions to the new pastor. He held his ground: "Why? Why do I need to keep that big bulb burning all the time?" "Well," his member responded, "you don't have to if you don't want to, but that's your pump house and if that light goes out, your water pipes will freeze and you won't have any water!" Welcome to the country, City Man! The journeys are different, but let's invite one another both to our common ground and to the riches of our various life expeditions.

The "view from the pew" is going to be formed by at least three principal dimensions, three lenses through which the view is formed. (1) People often play old tapes to form images of parsonage life.[10]

Memories of childhood can shape the way we look at things now. (2) The pastor and pastor's family send signals about their own expectations of and experiences of parsonage life. Is it always "open house" at the parsonage? Is the parsonage considered a personal enclave? Is money no object? Is there a false economy in not doing needed repairs? (3) Congregational lay leaders apprise the membership of the place of the parsonage in church life, church finances, and pastoral relationships. A good way to reflect on these items is to ask, *How does the parsonage express our congregational missional statement?*

Key to a view from the pew and a view from the pulpit is trust of each other. Do we both have the best interests of the other at heart? What can I do that will help you trust me? What do I need from you in order to trust you? Answering those questions becomes a worthy undertaking both in pew and in pulpit.

CHAPTER 9

LAST DAY AT THE PARSONAGE

Whether a move comes after a year or after ten years, there are memories to be packed with the books and clothes and dishes. Closure to a pastoral relationship can be difficult. Good-bye to friends. Good-bye to schoolmates. Good-bye to neighbors. Good-bye to familiar ways and familiar places. Good-bye to those who once welcomed you here. Good-bye to that Easter sunrise service breakfast better than any other in the region. Good-bye to that exciting new work mission project just beginning. Good-bye to that creative midweek worship service. Good-bye to the member who frequently called at 3:00 A.M. to say that he was sorry he had been drinking too much. Good-bye to the controversy over the color of the carpet in the sanctuary. Good-bye to the washing machine that flooded the parsonage weekly. Good-bye to the woman whose bagpipe practice woke you up on your day to sleep late. Good-bye to the high-speed Internet connection the church provided. Good-bye to the ghastly lamp you had to pull out of the closet if you saw its donor coming up the walk. Good-bye to the built-in grill in the backyard. Good-bye.

Leaving a parsonage is part of the mixture of feelings when it is time for a pastoral change. Recollections both happy and horrid fill the bank of family conversation. ("Do you remember the time they found that horse sleeping in the backyard?" "Do you remember the time I was sick and the church folks brought sitters around the clock so you could keep on working?" "Do you remember the time Puffy confused the Christmas box for her litter box?" "Do you remember the time we had the whole youth group here for a cookout and made that eighteen-inch hamburger?") Each parsonage adds to life's storehouse.

Most advisors offer one sentence of advice to pastors about leaving a parsonage: "Leave it cleaner than you found it." That might be easier said than done, given the trash and dirt and mud that can accumulate when moving. In recent moves, we got out of the house a couple of days early, stored our things on a truck—rented or moving company's—and then spent the night at a motel. (We figured this was our expense. Such a practice cleared the house for a wall-to-wall examination and polishing and allowed the congregation a brief respite before the new family arrived.

When finances allowed it, we figured it money well spent to have professional cleaners do the final touch).

Staying out of the house for a day or two before leaving (or just camping at the house with sleeping bags) assists with the timing concern: Are you going to be gone when your successor shows up? This is not as delicate a matter if there is going to be a search process to find the next pastor, but in those traditions in which outgoing and incoming clergy move on the same day, "getting out of Dodge" in a timely way is important!

In moving, you will be leaving some things you might like to take with you. For heaven's sake, don't! It is easy to become so accustomed to using a parsonage item that over a period of time you forget to whom it actually belongs. It is helpful to have a checklist of things that are property of the church (and mark those things so moving helpers do not misunderstand what goes and what stays), so there is no worry about "what ever happened to that desk lamp."

It is hard to leave behind shrubs and plants and gardens you have established. Know that the next family might not like roses and will dig up the roses you so carefully tended for four years. It happens. Even if they do not like squash, they might appreciate inheriting a well-weeded, prospering vegetable (or flower) garden. (Once when moving from a rural appointment, we inquired of our successor if he wanted us to get a garden started. He did and we did.)

Although it is not primarily your responsibility, collegiality suggests that you make certain that the congregation is preparing an appropriate welcome for the next pastor.[1] A clean house might be the best welcome! (I just spoke with a friend who moved this week to a new assignment. "I could have planted collards[2] in this parsonage," he said, noting how dirty the house was. Not only did he and his wife have the work of leaving a clean parsonage; they got double duty because they had to clean the one into which they moved.) Making sure the house is clean might be your best role in welcoming the next pastor.

There will be persons from the flock you are leaving who will want to help you move. (Of course, their motives in wanting to help might be varied. It is one way to make sure you get out of town!) Some of these helpers will volunteer to go with you on moving day to your new parsonage. As grateful as one is for such support, it might suggest to the receiving congregation that the new pastor has doubts about its welcome and its ability to provide backup for moving. Am I being too sensitive to think that moving day should belong fully to the new congregation?

Those who have moved with some regularity know that certain items are "pack in the car" items. The last day can be less harried if along the way the family has prepared a list of things to carry in the car. Delicate houseplants? Clothes for overnight? Important personal papers? Your pet tarantula? Aunt Patricia's antique vase? Computer? Artwork? Oh, yes— the children?[3] Cooler with drinks and snacks? The sermon for next Sunday? Fragile items? One guideline for deciding what goes into the car might be the proverbial question: What would you grab if the house caught on fire?

One thoughtful way to leave a parsonage (particularly if your successor is moving in on the same day) is to put down notes for the next pastor. For example, would she need to know that the mystery light switch by the door operates a bulb in the basement? How about the fact that the dishwasher will run only if the start button is pressed twice? When is garbage pickup day—or where is the county dump? How about emergency numbers: car repairs, physicians, friendly bank, nearest full-service grocery, nearest convenience mart? Is there a list of persons who are in the hospital? How about the names of people who have recently suffered a family loss? (There are many things that a pastorally responsible person will want to pass on to a successor. Perhaps your denomination has a checklist. If not, touch base with an experienced pastor.) Would it help to know that only items plugged into the top electrical socket will work when the wall switch is turned on? Have you gathered all the appliance manuals? How about leaving your new phone number in case you can help the new parsonage family resolve the confusion of a garage door opener that works if held in the right hand but not if held in the left hand? If you are the neat sort, these lists can be placed into a notebook. If you are the more relaxed sort, these lists can be scattered around the house in appropriate spots. (Once I knew my successor greatly loved a particular soft drink. I hid a few bottles of the beverage in places where he would find them as he unpacked.)

What about saying good-bye to people? Most of this will have occurred in other settings in your last few days at the church.[4] The last day is going to be packed enough (so to speak) without too many rounds of farewell moments. (Feelings can get hurt and leave a bitter taste of your pastorate if your last day visiting includes Person A but not Person B. Obviously, immediate neighbors, persons with follow-up responsibilities, and staff colleagues might need a final word.) With whom do you leave the parsonage keys? That might be a good spot for the last leave-taking.

If the house is going to be vacant for some time, take care of concerns such as electricity and gas. I know of a pastor whose parsonage burned the day his family moved in. Somewhere, I bet there is one whose parsonage burned on the day of departure. Is there a furnace running? Is there an air-conditioning unit on a timer? Is there a pilot light on the gas logs? What about the refrigerator? (If no one is moving in immediately, what is the best way to leave the refrigerator and freezer?)

There once was a baseball manager (Bobby Valentine of the New York Mets, if I remember correctly) who was kicked out of a game by the umpire. Later in the game, the manager tried to sneak back into the dugout, wearing a fake mustache, big glasses, and a different hat. It did not work. He was suspended and had to pay a fine. Kicked out or leaving under more pleasant circumstances, the departing pastor should stay departed. Most of us have little awareness of the unnecessary complications we can bring when we visit a former parish. (The current pastor is probably too polite to tell us.) Our very presence reminds members of "better days" or "worse days" or "good ol' days"—none of which is a helpful context in which the present pastor can work. Certainly we would not be so arrogant as to think the ministry of Jesus Christ is absent because we are absent! The last day at the parsonage is a clear sign that it is the last day of your ministry at Saint Gooseberry by the Wheatfield. Of course, the last day is emotional (negatively or positively). Of course, it is fraught with uncertainty. Of course, it is exhausting. Of course, it is closure. Of course, it is stressful. But it is a necessary part of the journey. Rejoice! God who came and tented among God's people (John 1:14)[5] takes that tent and moves with us!

In the following chapter, there are suggestions for prayers and family liturgy that can be a part of the last day at the parsonage. (There are also thoughts about other parsonage days: first day, open house, new house, renovated house, no longer a parsonage, and so forth.)

There may well be folks from the congregation at the parsonage to see you off (and to get things ready for the next pastor).[6] Hugs and hand-shakes (and tears) may help this moment, but at some point the family must get into the car and drive away. There is joy and expectancy in knowing that another group of God's family waits.[7]

CHAPTER 10

PARSONAGE PRAYERS

The pastor's work is immersed in prayer. Should not the pastor's home also be an avenue in the City of Prayer? This chapter offers prayers and liturgy that can be used in a variety of parsonage situations: first day, last day, open house, new house, renovated house, badly damaged or destroyed house, no longer a parsonage.

These are times primarily of family prayer. If there are children in the home, they can share in these moments. If it seems fitting, members of the pastoral advisory committee or parsonage committee might join in these prayer times. A pastor might well choose to complete these prayer disciplines alone. Feel free to use, adapt, and, alas, even ignore these suggestions. (Often, denominational worship books have additional resources.)

First Day at the Parsonage

Let those who will take part in these moments gather in a central place in the house: for example, den, kitchen, or front porch.

The family might sing a favorite hymn.

Read Matthew 5:14-16.

Pray: O God of new beginnings, you have been with us as we have left our old home, and now you greet us as we come to our new home. The days ahead are marked with uncertainty, but will surely contain joy and goodness because the days ahead contain your presence. Let your light shine in all that we do here and all that we are here.

Thank you for your ministry in this new place. Thank you for those who have labored here before us. Grant us the grace to nurture seeds they have planted in love. Bind our hearts to those with whom we now share common life. Bless the people of this congregation. As they have opened the doors of this parsonage to us, may we open the doors of our hearts to them.

Now move with benediction upon the rooms of this house. [You might choose to go from room to room as you offer this part of the prayer.] May the places of relaxation restore us to the mission of Jesus Christ. May the rooms for food remind us of the banquet in your coming kingdom. May the spaces of sleep and rest become spaces for your renewing goodness.

May the halls and hearth become places of hospitality. May the rooms for study become markets of insight and energy. In all ways, in all stages, may this place become home.

In the name of the One who had no place to lay his head, we offer this prayer of gratitude and readiness. Amen.

Last Day at the Parsonage

Perhaps these times of memory and prayer might best be observed by the parsonage family and the closest of friends. It includes a kind of late walk through this house that has been home. Tears and laughter may be your companions!

Sing these two stanzas by Charles Wesley (or read them aloud):

> Glory to God, and praise and love
> be ever, ever given,
> by saints below and saints above,
> the church in earth and heaven.
>
> O for a thousand tongues to sing
> my great Redeemer's praise,
> the glories of my God and King,
> the triumphs of his grace!

Read 2 Corinthians 13:11.

Begin this prayer in the area that has been the family's main gathering space. Invite family members to share special recollections of what has happened here. Then pray: Gracious God, you have been present with us here when times have been good. We also claim your call upon us and your nourishing attendance when times have not been good. Through it all we are grateful for love, both present and hoped for. Through Jesus Christ our Lord. Amen.

Invite the group (or yourself, if you are praying without others nearby) to move to one of the closets. Welcome any stories related to what has been kept in the closets of the house. Then pray: Loving God, in Jesus Christ has come a light that shines in all our darkness. Yet these storage spaces remind us of the times we have tried to hide from you and avoid your will. Hear our confession and restore us to holy living. Through Jesus Christ our Lord. Amen.

Now go into the areas where food has been prepared and served. What reminiscences come to mind of special meals, sad holidays, favorite foods, good times, rushed suppers, empty tables, and so forth? Then pray: Holy One, who at Emmaus was known to disciples in the breaking of bread, we know that you meet your people at table. We are grateful for hands and hearts that have made ready food in this place. We are thankful for those who have shared it with us. We are aware that some of the life at this space cannot be found again in another place, so we thank you for the blessing of our having been here. Through Jesus Christ our Lord. Amen.

Move to the area where guests have slept: a guest bedroom, a sofa, a floor for sleeping bags or inflatable mattresses.[1] Let family members recall things that have happened when company came. Did a visiting preacher take over a child's room? Did a favorite cousin come for two weeks every summer? Did the girls at a sleepover once spill all the water from the gold-fish bowl? Talk about it. Then pray: Our hearts fill with laughter and with tears as we recall those who have been guests in this home. We know, O Lord, that for you there are no near and far places, and that every place can be a place of home when we welcome you. Thank you for friends and family who have shared life in this parsonage. Heal any broken relationships with a fresh start. Keep alive any joy we have had with one another. Through Jesus Christ our Lord. Amen.

Now move to a bedroom or perhaps a hallway that opens into several family bedrooms. Point out that a bedroom is a very private space, an area one often describes as "my" bedroom. Out of respect for one another's privacy, let these times of recall be experienced silently. Then, pray: Blessed Savior, we come now to places where there have been loving, warming thoughts, but also sometimes hostile and bitter words. Here, as much as anywhere, we have been our real selves. And still you have loved us! Thank you that we have had a roof over our heads and, more than that, we have had the shelter of your protection. Through Jesus Christ our Lord. Amen.

Finally, go to other places in the parsonage that have been important to the family: a garage, a study, a workshop, a play area, a garden, even a bathroom. Offer people a chance to remember how these spots have been particularly meaningful. Then, pray: Gifts such as these, O Lord, may be only for a season. We acknowledge that sometimes our happiness has been flecked with disappointment; sometimes our hope has been met with faltering. But, for better and for worse, this has been home. Now we release it for the ministry of others. And we move to another place where you wait for us, so we can taste even now the final home you have made for us. Through Jesus Christ our Lord. Amen.

Open House at the Parsonage[2]

Before the guests begin to arrive, gather the parsonage family (and any helpers) for this prayer: Dear Lord, who enjoyed the hospitality at the home of Zacchaeus, who came to a party with the tax collector and with the Pharisees, who was fully present at the wedding in Cana of Galilee, and who went home with the men met on the road to Emmaus; Jesus, our Redeemer, you invite us to come as family to your table and there to eat and drink of the grain and fruit of life; you tell us of a banquet at which all of your kin will have food and fellowship. So now we come to these moments of open house in the spirit of your welcome and in the assurance of your presence.

Bless those who come as guests. As they share in this our home, may they also share in the love of the one in whose name this place is built and in whose grace this house is maintained.

Always keep us mindful of your children who have no place to call home. Let the openness of the parsonage become a sign of our mission to be your arms and legs in ministry to the homeless.

Grant us now gifts of calmness and use our preparations as ways to honor your name and give care to your people. Through Jesus Christ our Lord. Amen.

Completion of Renovation[3]

Even if there is not a major churchwide celebration of the renovation of the parsonage, such a completion might be the occasion for a smaller observance. Perhaps the parsonage committee and key church officials might join the family in this prayer time.

The pastor and the chair of the project could begin by offering words of appreciation for those who saw the need and those who planned and implemented ways to meet the need.[4] Then this prayer could be led by one of the laypeople:

O God, whose grace is always sufficient, we thank you for the good thing you have done in our midst. You have raised up servants who look with caring eyes and with willing hands. You have planted in our hearts a desire to move from what is to what can be. You have given us the means with which we have undertaken this venture of improvement. Our hearts fill with gratitude and we commit ourselves to lives of grateful living.

Pour blessing upon our parsonage family. Move with peace that this home may be a place of peace. Come with love that this home may be a place of love. Come with joy that this home may be a place of joy. Hear our gratitude for the one who serves us as pastor. Hear our thankfulness for those others gathered here whose support gives strength to ministry and whose struggles give occasions for growth.

Turn these things of wood and brick and paint into expressions of caring, and move us all toward the perfect love granted us in Jesus Christ, in whose name we pray. Amen.

Moving Day

Consider placing this prayer in a church bulletin or newsletter so the entire congregation can be in prayer on moving day. In those denominations in which one pastor moves out and another moves in on the same day, this is a two-edged prayer. The moving pastors can have the power of this prayer support even (particularly?) from persons who are not even near the parsonage on moving day.

Prayer for Moving Day: On this day, O Lord, we your children pray for pastors everywhere. Grant them courage of conviction, clarity of expression, and warmth of relationship. Watch over our shepherds as they move this day. For one who has been among us, we pray for traveling mercies and the bounty of a good tomorrow. For one who comes to us, we pray for traveling mercies and the bounty of a good tomorrow. Use us as instruments of your hospitality so that in all things and in all ways, we become one family fulfilling your healing and saving purposes through Jesus Christ, in whose name we pray. Amen.

Opening of a New Parsonage

There are services for the blessing of a home (including a parsonage) in the worship resource books of various traditions.[5] Such occasions are good settings for inviting colleagues from other congregations, from other denominations, and from the broader denomination of the host congregation.

If a full service of worship is desired, the planning team might consider having it at the church building, and then moving to the parsonage for a briefer time of consecration. (Exactly where would you seat 300 people at the parsonage!) Congregations who do not anticipate unmanageable numbers would, of course, think of having the entire service at the new parsonage.

As in any building project, the parsonage needs to be cleared for occupancy. If it is not ready when the long-scheduled day appears, temporary one-time approval may be granted by the county, state, municipality, or whoever makes that decision in your community. If worse comes to worst, hold all of the service outside the new house and let the pastor and family wear construction hard hats and make a ceremonial entrance![6]

Because there are so many prayer resources for the consecration or dedication of a new parsonage, my suggestion here is for a prayer that could be used at a meeting of those planning the service.

Prayer: O God, the Creator of all things, we praise your name for working your creative spirit in the midst of this congregation. You have blessed us with a vision and have granted us the energy, focus, and tools to move toward that goal. As we come now to the fulfillment of our dream of a new parsonage, we give you the honor and glory. Move in our minds and hearts that we might be led to ways of celebration that will inspire, to moments of commitment that will renew, and to generosity of spirit that will grow. Free us from personal agenda and clear our path of broken places that as one family we can with delight enjoy what you have done among us. Bless our pastor even as we thank you for his (her) patience, understanding, and now, readiness! Keep us ever mindful of those who have no home and let our gladness grow legs of service and witness, through Jesus Christ our Lord. Amen.

Closing a Parsonage

Occasionally, a congregation comes to a decision to stop using a particular house as its parsonage. It is a common practice to have services to deconsecrate a church building, but why not also a service to close out use of a parsonage?

Such a gathering might be tied into a homecoming weekend. Former pastors who lived in the parsonage could be invited. (Returning to a previous pastorate makes sense when all former pastors are asked to come for an event.) If the parsonage has served the church for decades, the history committee might want to prepare a display: photographs over the years and a story of how the house was built. Frequently, there are memories of fund-raising events and special campaigns "so we could have a parsonage."

Ideally, a "house retirement" service would include time at the former parsonage. If it has been sold and the new family is living there, careful negotiation and open cooperation would be needed.[7] The ideas below may need a great deal of tweaking to work in any particular situation, but give some thought to a service "to let go of" a parsonage no longer needed.

Begin with a hymn such as "O God, Our Help in Ages Past" or "Now Thank We All Our God."

Follow with a statement of purpose for this ceremony: "My brothers and sisters, we come together because God has moved this congregation to a new moment in its journey. This parsonage has been home for our pastors for thirty-five years. We have a new parsonage, duly set aside to give a place of domestic strength to those who come to serve among us. We come to this time, to this place, to give thanks to God for the days, weeks, months, and years that have been shaped and fed by the lives lived out here."

Leader: God has been good to us.

Response: Thanks be to God.

Leader: God has sent us shepherds of the flock.

Response: Thanks be to God.

Leader: God has allowed us to care for the shepherds.

Response: Thanks be to God.

Leader: God has used this house as a home for our pastors.

Response: Thanks be to God.

Leader: O God, whose mercy is never-failing, blow the winds of fresh grace upon us that we might enjoy now moments of good memory, times of healed relationships, blessings of new experiences. We thank you for those women and men who have been our pastors. We are grateful for the families who brought variety and growth among us. We express thankful hearts for the days here of shelter, of challenge, of truth, of peace, of home. For a season, this has been a place set apart. Now we release this house into other uses. As we take it from its special place in our congregation's life, continue to touch and bless those who live here. Your Word has taught us that unless you build a house, those who build it labor in vain (Psalm 127:1a), so we dare to proclaim that you have built this house, for its work and its play have been acts of your mission. Thank you for those whose sacrificial giving made possible this parsonage. Receive our gratitude for their generosity as our own commitment for the days ahead, and we shall give you all the praise. Through Jesus Christ our Lord. And all God's people said,

Response: Amen!

If time allows, encourage members and former pastors to share memories of the former parsonage. After each one speaks, the gathered people could respond: "God has been here! Thanks be to God!"[8]

Are there enough people to encircle the house for the benediction? If so, let the leader start and each one, in sequence, pass to his or her neighbor the words "May Christ go with you." If there are not enough to surround the building, invite those present to touch some portion of the building as the leader says: "Go forth to tomorrow. Bring with you the gifts of yesterday and claim fully the power of this moment. And the blessing of the triune God go with us all, now and forevermore. Amen."

If there has been some distinctive item of historic value in the parsonage (a large Bible that was always at the parsonage or a significant painting, for example), you could include a ritual for "leave-taking" with this object to take it to the new parsonage.

CHAPTER 11

IN CONCLUSION

The late James McCallum told about listening to a commencement speaker who had lost his terminating facilities. The speech droned on and on. Restless graduates began to shuffle to try to find the elusive comfortable spot in the hard seats. More talk. Blah. Blah. Blah. Finally, ears and interest perked up when the orator said, "So, in conclusion, let me say...." Ears and interest both shut down as the windy presenter continued, "In conclusion, let me say preliminarily...."

This is the concluding chapter of this book, but maybe that graduation speaker had the right idea. The conclusion is really just a different stage in the preliminaries. There is always more, a next step.

This eye to the changing days sends us a clear signal: parsonages today are not like they were fifty years ago, and fifty years from now they will not be like they are today.[1] In some parts of the country, there is a trend toward replacing parsonages with housing allowances. (It would not surprise me to see that direction reverse. Maybe the move will be toward houses rented as parsonages, giving flexibility to all concerned.) So, these last chapter conclusions might not be so conclusive after all.

Eugenia (another made-up name) recounts a parsonage life that captures much of the journey of these pages. As she and her pastor husband prepared to move, their neighbor came over with a cat. It was a feline they had shared with the people next door, and now the neighbor wanted to give the cat fully to Eugenia. "This cat always loved you more than it did me." Eugenia accepted the "gift," but when she tried to place the cat into a carrier, the shy animal bit her. The move must go on, so they departed (cat in cage) to their next parsonage assignment.

A welcoming parsonage committee greeted Eugenia and Pastor Enrico, ready to serve the tired travelers a meal. Eugenia went to a side porch to try to settle down the newly acquired family pet, but when her husband opened the porch door, the cat bolted. Gone! Out the door in a flash!

Eugenia went in full pursuit after the disappearing feline. ("I had not even had a chance to greet the parsonage committee and to thank them for the food.") She sped across the parsonage backyard and into the yard of the new neighbors. As she was crawling around under the neighbor's shrubbery, the neighbor came out and brusquely asked, "Could I help you?" Eugenia smiled and said, "No, thank you. I'm just looking!" (Then she laughed and told her what she was doing.) Having not found the cat—it was never seen again—Eugenia went back to the parsonage, greeted the committee, and thanked them for their hospitality.

Enrico went to the church to set up his office. Eugenia decided to go alone to an urgent care facility to get a tetanus shot for that cat bite. While she was there, her blood sugar level dropped and Eugenia blacked out. The doctor would not let her drive, so her husband had to get a church member to drive him to the doctor's office so he could drive Eugenia's car back to the parsonage. "What a grand entrance! What a great first impression! But those people were so gracious and loved us, in spite of my messy beginning!"

That was only a start. On day three at the parsonage, Eugenia was glad to see that evidently action was being taken on some repairs needed at the house. After she had mopped water each day, she was delighted to see the plumber at the door. He began work on a downstairs half-bath. "I told him the bathroom was fine and did not need fixing, but he said he would 'change it out anyway.'" When Eugenia went to the basement to do a load of wash, she was startled by a shower falling on the clothes she was sorting. She ran upstairs and found the floor of the half-bath immersed in running water, which was now leaking down to the basement. She turned the knobs under the commode and called the plumber to return. And she mopped some more.

When Eugenia got back to the basement to continue her washing project, she reset the machine before it started its spin cycle. She gently opened the lid to put the clothes into the unit—and boom! Zip! The washing machine agitator flew out of the machine, taking off as a rocket might. (Shades of a runaway cat!) Eugenia suggests that her remarks at this point might not be fit for a book published by this fine publisher, but she reports that it all turned out OK.

The next day, the chairperson of the parsonage committee came by to say that the church was going to paint, carpet, remodel, and replace as needed! No wonder Eugenia closes her notes on those early days in this parsonage by writing, "All in all, I feel that the parsonage system is wonderful. It is great not to have to look for a house and wonder where you are going to live. It is also great not to have to move a lot of furniture. The people we served have always been willing to work with us and did all they could to make us comfortable and, truth to tell, we were."

Do you notice the pattern of mutuality in Eugenia's account? The parsonage "worked" because the congregation wanted to do what was best for the pastor and family; the parsonage family was patient and open and grateful. The feeling here is not one of unhealthy dependency, but is one of common mission: *What does each of us need to do in order for this arrangement to work for both of us?*

Sometimes it does not work.[2] When that happens, both pastor and congregation need to consume massive doses of accountability, forgiveness, and openness. Sometimes an angry pastor or an angry congregation is hearing the tapes of previous bad experiences. The unfortunate beginning assumption in those cases is that parsonages are about "we" and "they." By way of contrast, when there is disagreement about a parsonage, a starting point might be a conversation about "on what do we agree?" Those spots of agreement can become the initial background for working through differences. "My way or the highway" is not the prime sentence for dialogue.

If need be, is there an outside entity that might help resolve parsonage dead-end streets?[3] Good questions might be: Are the issues about taste or about safety? Are the obstacles due to financial considerations or to lack of priority? How could the unmet need be provided for in some other way? (One church member gave the pastor's family a key to the member's lake house so they could get away when they wanted to.) In what ways has the parsonage stress made ministry less effective (by the pastor? by the congregation?)? What are potential positions for compromise? ("Let's store the church's bedroom suite, but let's use the parsonage living room furniture.") Recognizing that a family is a system, which family members seem to be the "rubbing point" in the system? What timetable can be set for action, and who will report to whom about actions taken? How will priorities be set for action? What mission in the name of Jesus Christ goes undone if the parsonage conflict remains unresolved?[4]

Parsonages become places of rest and recovery and nourishment and nurture (they become "home") when congregation and pastor understand that they really are on the same side! One colleague has shared this account of how she and her congregation did ministry together in a time of personal predicament. She marked her memory this way: "Two months after I moved to the Centerville Charge[5] I broke my ankle. For the next two months, I was in a cast, unable to put my foot on the floor for four weeks. Within days of my breaking the ankle, I was responsible for the first funeral since I had come to that charge. A nurse in the congregation came and helped me bathe and dress. Two men came to drive me and my wheelchair to the church; they carried me in my wheelchair into the pulpit so I could officiate at that service. One woman drove me every-where I needed to go. Another brought me breakfast and my mail every day. Someone else came and got the bulletin material to take to the print shop. Yet another came to do the laundry. One appeared at my door with the announcement, 'I have come to do your ironing.' For two weeks, folks showed up at the parsonage every day to feed the family. I preached twice every Sunday and never missed a service at any of my three congrega-tions. I even preached the homecoming sermon in a church where my father had once been pastor; I did it standing on one foot while propping on crutches! I learned how to let my congregation minister to me!"

That can happen when all recognize that the ministry is what we have in common! Of course, persons who do not live in a parsonage can tell similar stories of support from friends. But that is the point: the pastor at Centerville was not viewed as an "other" but as "one of us." It was not because she was so dearly loved (after all, she had only been there two months when she broke the ankle), but because the congregations knew that they shared the work of ministry with whoever their pastor might be. They loved the human contents of the parsonage![6]

How about the congregation that put up a fence after the pastor's two-year-old son bounded into the road on moving day? How about the parish-ioner who loaned his own house to the pastor's family when an ice storm led to a malfunctioning oil heater at the parsonage?[7] What about the pastor who kept in good spirits by naming an unvented portable space heater "Agnes" after a member who also gurgled? What about the parsonage family who had to hide the first batch of donated garden vegetables so as not to offend the folks who brought the second batch of donated fresh vegetables? What about one daughter of a parsonage who as a mature adult still hesitates to shop on Sunday "for fear someone will know I am the preacher's daughter"? What about the parsonage family who somehow managed to show appreci-ation for the live turkey that was delivered to the parsonage as a treat on Christmas morning? How about the man who climbed on the parsonage roof on a cold winter day so "the preacher can have as good TV reception as the rest of us"? What about the pastor who always asked, "Will the next pastor like this?" when facing parsonage decisions?

Any book on parsonage life is bound to stir hearts, reframe old ques-tions, invoke earlier hurts, celebrate victories of grace, and give evidence that we are still on the road to perfection. It might be "their house," but it is "my home." The gifts and the tensions of that reality become the set-ting in which God continues to pour grace, abundant grace, sufficient grace. Thanks be to God!

NOTES

Introduction

1. Although Oscar is in every sense of the word a wonderful name for a cat, I am more impressed by the United Methodist clergy family who bravely named its dog "Bishop." This appellation lent itself to many splendid occasions of advising the "Bishop," reproving the "Bishop," and even, alas, kicking the "Bishop." This arrangement worked well until the real live episcopal leader came to visit at the parsonage. Having anticipated some possible canine confusion, the family lent the cocker spaniel to the protection of a neighbor's fenced-in yard. Good plan, right? Well, it was a good plan until the dear ecclesiastical pomp was on the front porch extending farewells to the family (who was breathing a sigh of relief at surviving this particular engagement). As the bishop began to climb into his car, the five-year-old son of the household ran to release his fenced-in pet. The four-legged Bishop was so thrilled at this freedom that she began to run away. The visiting prelate, readying to depart, was a bit flummoxed by the sound of the shouts of the five-year-old: "Don't leave, Bishop! Come back, Bishop! You know what I'll do if I get my hands on you, Bishop!" No further comment seems necessary.

2. The late John Rudin taught me the word "persiflage." Unfortunately, he used it in the context of describing my leadership at a staff meeting. Look it up. You will find "persiflage" a valuable addition to your arsenal of ministry tools.

3. And then there is the one about the taciturn local who was asked if he had lived all his life in this community. "Not yet," he replied.

4. Something of warmth is lost in the New Revised Standard Version translation of Jonah 4:11. In the King James Version (copies of which can still be found in many parsonage living room end table drawers), that verse describes the people of Nineveh as those "who cannot discern between their right hand and their left hand; and also much cattle." This does not have anything in particular to do with our topic, but I recognize in a mirror the part about not knowing the left hand from the right hand!

5. Perhaps you know that 86.4% of statistics are made up on the spot. In that spirit, I report that a recent survey revealed that 61.8% of parsonages had the colonial painting "Sunday Morning" hanging in the living room. Further research, equally valid no doubt, says that within two weeks of a pastoral change, the painting is relocated to safe storage, preferably out of view.

6. One brother of the cloth has described a parsonage encounter with another of God's special creatures, the mouse. He lived with his wife in an apartment rented as the parsonage for him when he was a student pastor. His report, quoted with anonymous permission, is: "One evening during dinner, my wife and I saw a mouse scamper across the kitchen floor. Being childless and unable to have pets in the apartment, we decided to adopt the mouse. We named it Speedy (after a cartoon mouse of the same name). We would put peanuts in a jar lid and watch Speedy come out, at first tentatively, and then with courage, grabbing a peanut and disappearing. One day I even found peanut shells in my shoes, giving me a hint as to where Speedy enjoyed his meals. We did fail to put out water for

71

Speedy, and that might have led to his demise. One morning, I went into the bathroom and discovered Speedy floating in the toilet. We determined that he had needed water so badly (salty peanuts?) that he chose the commode as his watering hole."

7. United Methodist pastors (and others in a system of ecclesiastical appointments) recognize that they might well end up in South Scintillating, East Downtown, West Boredom, or North Nowhere without any final say in the matter. Although such clergy might be consulted, they have agreed to a structure in which someone else makes the decision as to where the pastor will live.

8. At a recent gathering of pastors, I asked how many lived in parsonages with green carpets. All but three raised a hand. Those three had beige carpets. Early parsonages, however, had no carpet: they ranged from dirt floors to bare wood. Green is good; it beats dirt.

9. For United Methodists, this understanding is stated clearly: Among the responsibilities of the Church Council is to "review the recommendation of the committee on pastor-parish relations regarding provision of adequate housing for the pastor(s), and report the same to the charge conference for approval. Housing provisions shall comply with the annual conference housing policy and parsonage standards. Housing shall not be considered as part of the compensation or remuneration" (*The Book of Discipline of The United Methodist Church 2004* [Nashville: United Methodist Publishing House, 2004], paragraph 252.4e).

10. *The Book of Discipline of The United Methodist Church 1988* (Nashville: United Methodist Publishing House, 1988), paragraph 256.3f. This concept—although the disciplinary wording no longer appears—seems to continue to define United Methodist understanding of housing for its pastors. Although I am no tax expert (feel free to underline this disclaimer!), I sense that tax law agrees with an awareness that parsonages are for the benefit of the church because current tax provisions allow pastors not to count as income anything spent on parsonage maintenance or supplies. Note well: this provision for housing exclusion allowance applies only to the clergyperson and would not be in effect for a surviving spouse. As footnotes usually say in advice columns, "consult with your professional tax advisor."

11. In the process of thinking about this book, I discovered that the Hungarian word for parsonage is *plébánia* and the Swedish word for parsonage is *prästgård*. For most readers, this information will have a fairly limited range of usefulness, but for those for whom it is important, it is *very* important.

1. Someone Else's House

1. Who actually holds legal title to the house varies according to denominational or local church polity. It might be the property of the congregation or in the name of a group of trustees or, as in the case of United Methodism, held by the local church (or charge) "in trust for The United Methodist Church and subject to the provisions of its *Discipline*" (*The Book of Discipline 2004*, paragraph 2501).

2. I recognize that "most" is a slippery word. Obviously, if you are the one whose home has been violated by aggressively controlling congregants, you think the word "most" is a bit of an overstatement. If you are a parishioner who has tried very hard over the years to respect the home life of the pastor's family, you will probably see yourself among the "most." When it comes to "most," perhaps my Presbyterian colleague James M. Efird is correct when he says, "You pay your money and you take your choice."

3. OK, since you insist, I'll tell you my almost horror story about insurance. I was in my fifth appointment before a helpful colleague told me about my needing personal insurance on my own worldly goods. "The church's insurance does not cover what you own." In light of his good advice, I bought some renter's insurance. Two weeks later, the phone rang at the church office. My son, just home from his day at school, said, "Uh, Dad, I think you might need to come home." This was an unusual word from our mature and self-sufficient eleventh grader.

"What's the problem?" I asked, trying to steel myself for the worst.

"The dining room ceiling is on the floor."

I went home. Plaster had failed in that grand room, and indeed the ceiling had collapsed onto the dining table (church property), had broken chairs (church property), had destroyed the chandelier (church property), had dented the floor (church property), had powdered the carpet (church property), had ripped the wallpaper (church property), had attacked the buffet and sideboard (church property), had smashed the silver service given us by a former church (oops! personal property), had broken an heirloom pitcher (oops! personal property), and had traumatized our fourteen-year-old beagle (double oops! personal "property"). The insurance did not do much for our dog—who can imagine what he thought when he heard this crashing in the room next to his bedding place in the kitchen!—but it did cover replacement and repair costs on our personal items. Had it not been for the renter's insurance (OK, I know I'm not renting the parsonage, but that is the category into which this coverage falls), we would have had only broken memories and a very nervous canine friend.

4. As far as I know, no one in my immediate family (or extended family, for that matter) is employed in the insurance business, but don't you think my insurance agent ought to give me a discount for encouraging all these people to buy insurance?

5. Once, on moving day, my predecessor asked if he could leave "a few things" in the parsonage storage space. I estimated quickly that the likelihood was small that the third of the basement he needed would ever be available for my use. I said, "No." I still feel guilty about that. What do you think I should have said?

6. Department of Disclaimer: check with your tax advisor. These laws tend to change from time to time, and they vary from state to state. With all due respect to Amos 7:14, I am neither a tax advisor nor the son of a tax advisor.

7. Toni and I did a two-step plan. Early on, we could not afford a retirement house (although we did have a pop-up camper trailer with a chest for ice), so we did what we could: we bought some land. It sat empty for years and years (with some very attractive weeds and wildflowers). After the land was paid for, we continued to set aside some coinage for a house. Just prior to retirement, we used those funds to make a down payment on the construction of a small house suited to our two-person household. If you are still making payments in retirement, try to have your life insurance coverage sufficient not to leave your family with huge house payments. "Some day, son, this will all be yours."

8. What is a major appliance? Is it simply one too heavy to move easily? Is it one more expensive than, say, an alarm clock? How about cable or satellite television? Phone service? Computer? Pipe organ? Lawnmower (riding or push)? Fax machine? Septic tank alarm system? I have heard heated—uh—engaging discussions about every one of those items except pipe organ. Very few parsonages—.005% (see note 5 in the Introduction section)—have pipe organs.

9. It is hard to imagine the heat that can be generated, so to speak, by a debate over

who fills up the oil tank! In a connectional system, a policy can be established that affects all congregations (such as, you find it full and you leave it full). In a congregational system, having an understanding in advance will help things get off to a better start—if everyone involved knows what that understanding is!

10. I have been waiting for a chance to unload this one: Did you hear about the fellow who said he did not know anything about rocks? (He said he just took them all for granite.)

2. First Day at the Parsonage

1. Here is a word of advice to any district superintendents (or other denominational semi-dignitaries) about visiting pastors on moving day. This early call is a noble gesture, appreciated by many clergy and dreaded by a few. If you are the superintendent, be sure to wear a very nice shirt and probably a tie or a frilly blouse with pearls.[1] If you are dressed in this fashion, surely no one will expect you to do any actual work, heavy lifting, or sweat-producing activity. Be sure to wave vigorously to the workers as you get back into your air-conditioned car. (In truth, many congregations and pastors value this visit, a signal that "the powers that be" know something important is happening in our congregation today.)

2. Several thousands of dollars? Probably not. It was more likely a few hundred dollars worth of damage, but if I am going to disguise this story to protect "JCN," I am certainly going to disguise the truth enough to make it a better story.

3. In some judicatories, arrangements are made for paying some, if not all, the moving expense of a pastor. This is one of those things that need to be clear before moving day!

4. One pastor's wife reports a next-door neighbor (a church member) who asked the clergy spouse, "How do you feel when you go to the grocery store and know you are spending money put in the offering plate?" Most of the appropriate answers to that inquiry are beyond the bounds of decorum and will not be discussed here.

5. This last question is made even more persuasive if you happen to be handling a small box with airholes at the time you speak. On the other hand, you might prefer to redirect your "helper's" attention by asking, "But could you tell me where the best grocery store in town is?" Or, "But could you help me remember the names of the folks who have helped today?" (Having the names of those who helped on moving day can help you write thank-you notes or remind you to include a "thanks" section in the church newsletter or bulletin.)

6. New pastors may need to open new checking accounts too. Is there a branch of your previous bank in the new community? One of my more embarrassing moments in one new appointment was being called by the local school and being told that my check for our son's school supplies had bounced. (Talk about a good first impression!) The school folks seemed to understand that I had tried to close out the bank account in my previous city by spending every penny in the account. Alas, my spending habits were more prolific than my arithmetic skills. There was only $4.32 to cover my check for $15.00. Don't you think "close" ought to count?

7. I did not want to insult any real pastor, so I made up the name "Brother Turkey." Then I checked the complete listing of all United Methodist clergy members of annual conferences. There is not one United Methodist pastor whose real name is Turkey. The alphabetical list goes from Turkelson to Turkington. Although I have never seen one, I cannot vouch for the presence or absence of Turkeys in other denominations.

8. Isn't "triangulation" what pastoral-care folks call it when someone (Person A) tries to get a third person (Person C) into the middle of a dispute between Person A and Person B? ("Reverend Sparks, Bill and I have been fussing about the color of the carpet in the nursery. What color do you think it ought to be?")

9. Extra advice on the side: pack everything you will need the first night in one box and carry it in the car. And never, never, never label a box "miscellaneous." (Most boxes get marked that way in the final hours of packing. I have found that most "miscellaneous" boxes stay in the attic unopened until it is time to move again.)

10. On one occasion, a colleague and I were "swapping" appointments: he was coming where I had been serving and I was going where he had been serving. Both assignments were in the same city, but parsonage swapping was also part of the arrangement. Coordinating this moving time was easy; I called and said, "We can leave in about fifteen minutes. Are you ready?" He replied, "Give us thirty minutes." The phone rang and he said, "We'll pull out of the driveway at 11:50." "Agreed!" It is the only time when Toni and I moved and were able actually to wave to our successors as we passed each other on the highway!

11. The unfortunate truth is that liquor boxes make some of the finest cartons available for moving. One point of interest is determining who will volunteer to go to the liquor store to obtain the boxes. Most moving pastors will hastily point out that they did not accumulate these useful containers in the course of normal refreshment.

12. Even in the wonderful days of yesteryear, few parsonages were as basic as a trailer. This particular parsonage was not a manufactured house; it was not a mobile home; it was not a double-wide; it was a trailer. If one sat on the couch, one's feet touched the opposite wall. The pastor had to stand in the hall to shave because the bathroom was not high enough for his six-foot two-inch frame. If it makes you feel any better, this first day happened in 1960.

13. If you do not know what chitlins are, may I suggest that you look it up. I don't have the intestinal fortitude, as it were, to tell you.

3. Goldfish and Preachers

1. The phrase "someone has said" often means "I don't want to take the blame for having said it."

2. Let the record show that I am pleased to be chaplain of the Fellowship Dartball League. For one thing, it means I get to go through the line first at the annual banquet. Of course, this special recognition is very embarrassing to me, but I try to bear up under the humiliation and enjoy the barbecued chicken, potato salad, and green beans. Of course, it is awkward to be going back for seconds when some people are still in line for their first bite.

3. Occasions for public prayers vary from region to region. Public prayers are strictly forbidden in some places, quietly expected in other places, and passionately sought in other places. Such times can test a pastor's mettle, such as when my friend was asked to pray at the dedication of his community's new sewage treatment facility.

4. Vacations are wonderful, but one pastor colleague told me that he never felt he got far enough away from his hometown to go to a Hooters restaurant. Being pure of heart, I did not know what he meant.

5. Department of My Guilt: When our family moved into one parsonage, we found a

metal sign in the front yard: "Methodist Parsonage." Mysteriously (?), the identifying sign disappeared in about two weeks.

6. At one such open house, we finally posted a family member at the master bedroom closet. Three or four people had commented on the size of the closet, which we translated to mean, "We enjoyed looking over your wardrobe." Perhaps we should have hidden our son in the closet to jump out at the next soul who ventured into this personal space.

7. The same pastor who told me of this exchange related a follow-up incident in which this church member tried to get into the goldfish bowl—uh, the parsonage—on her own. The pastor and his wife had announced that they were leaving town on Saturday for a wedding anniversary trip. Their departure was delayed briefly by a pastoral emergency at the hospital, so the pastor's wife went with him so they could leave from the hospital as soon as he finished his call there. The short hospital visit turned into a long hospital visit; and by the time the pastor could leave the hospital, he and his wife wanted to run back by the parsonage to freshen up for the journey. Upon returning home, they noticed a car in the driveway, the car belonging to the woman who had asked to be invited to the parsonage for meetings. The parsonage side door was not visible from the street, so the pastor parked the car on the road and walked quietly to the side entrance. The woman's back was turned and she did not hear nor see the pastor until he spoke her name. She had the key in the lock, had opened the door, and was about to walk in when the pastor spoke her name. She jumped in surprise. "Can I help you with anything?" the good reverend asked. "Why, yes, you can," she answered. "I just came by to deliver this anniversary card! Happy anniversary!" The pastor wondered out loud why the visitor had not simply put the card into a mailbox. "That would spoil the surprise." Surprise, indeed. The anniversary trip was delayed another two hours as the beleaguered pastor and wife took time to go to the hardware store to get a new set of locks for all the parsonage entry doors.

8. One colleague told this story of fiery parsonage passion. He had saved all the steamy love letters he and his wife-to-be had exchanged during courtship. During the more practical years of later marriage (how sad!), his spouse decided that she was not comfortable with those letters remaining for children and grandchildren to use for jokes at family reunions. "Burn them!" she urged her pastor husband. The good brother dutifully threw the entire box into the woodstove, hoping to encourage the heat box to even greater outbursts of heat. Unfortunately, the creosote build-up in the chimney took this occasion to catch a spark and send plumes of (romantic) dark soot and flames pouring out into the night air. "I didn't even know the house was on fire until the fire truck pulled into the yard," the pastor reports. Thankful that someone was keeping an eye on the parsonage, he appreciated this invasion of privacy! (Oh, yes. The letters burned up, but the marriage has remained a splendid multi-decadal venture.)

9. Some years ago, seeing the grass grow much higher than usual prompted one parishioner to check on a pastor who was single. No one had seen him for several days. His out-of-town son came when called and together they found the pastor had died alone at the parsonage.

4. Family Fabric

1. A veterinarian once told me that a cat does not have an appendix. This arrangement seems highly unfair either to our feline friends or to us. I'm just not sure which.

2. A favorite story in my family is about my grandmother, "Mama Joyner." She was

married to a plainspoken Methodist pastor, but she was not given much to public expressions of her faith. Once at a revival, the guest preacher noted my grandmother in the congregation and called on her to pray. Then. Aloud. "Mrs. Joyner, will you lead us in prayer?" Mama Joyner was chagrined at this open request that she pray in front of the whole assemblage, so she turned to the woman sitting next to her and, looking for a substitute prayer-giver, whispered, "Would you pray for me?" The neighbor agreed, rose to her feet, and intoned, "O Lord, bless Mrs. Joyner. Keep her in your care. Watch over her, and whatever be the burden she is bearing now, stay with her. Amen." At least, you can say she was prayed for.

3. If I really knew the answer to this question, don't you think I would be running a counseling service in my retirement instead of writing books?

4. The really deeply satisfying responses are probably best said only to the mirror. Unless you know how to express your true emotions in some obscure foreign language that no one will recognize, you best tone down the vocabulary of your responses!

5. I hope you don't mind, but my favorite joke (at the moment) does not really fit into this discussion. Is it OK if I tell it anyhow? A man goes into the doctor's office and says, "Doctor, I need to see you. I think I am a moth." The physician replied, "Sir, I don't think I can help you. I am a general practitioner; you should see a psychiatrist." "Oh, indeed," the man replied. "I was on my way to my psychiatrist's office but your light was on."

6. A case can be made that where the parsonage children go to school is nobody's business except the parsonage family's. Nevertheless, it does not hurt a pastor's strength in leadership if he or she shows sensitivity to things that matter to the self-image or self-understanding of the members of the congregation. If schooling is a sticky question, it is best to keep the discussion on top of the table rather than having misunderstandings.

7. OK, they told me it was a dog, but it was the ugliest canine I have ever seen. To me it looked more like a duck-billed platypus.

8. These ruminations are dedicated to Frisky (a basement and outdoor otterhound), to Snoopy (a kitchen, porch, and outdoor beagle), to Pommes Frites (a kitchen playpen and fenced-in outside Dalmatian), and to Al (a cat that never came inside after taking up with us and so named as short for "allergy" for obvious—ah choo!—reasons).

9. Uh, this is particularly important if your pet is a horse. Hmmm.

10. A small baby playpen can work. Pommes Frites (his full name was Sir Walter Pommes Frites) was a sixty-five-pound Dalmatian. He stayed in the floorless pen from day one and always thought that inside life (mostly for sleep) was pen-shaped. He did his romping in the fenced-in yard (we paid for the fencing) or when on a leash.

11. A cat without claws needs to become a permanent inside resident. The truth of the matter is, de-clawing is now frowned upon by many cat-lovers, and numerous veterinarians even refuse to perform the procedure. Check with your cat, your conscience, and your vet!

12. The real point here is that some word from your previous appointment might allay some fears at your new appointment. This would not mean that your guinea pig is a pork barrel project.

13. This choice falls into the "these dogs are like my children" category. Pets can indeed be like members of the family. Ask yourself: "Can I not be effective for Jesus Christ unless this family pet is at hand?" Balance your covenants: Weigh the pastoral covenant and the family covenant and the stewardship covenant for all of creation. Sometimes these things weigh more than we thought they might.

14. Most of us would not choose a home where the buffalo roam, whether or not the skies are cloudy all day.

15. PK is a classic abbreviation for "Preacher's Kid" or "Parsonage Kid." Our son preferred "TO": theologian's offspring.

5. *The Toilet Seat Doesn't Work*

1. "Karen" is not Joyce's real name. (Joyce is not her name either!)

2. Repairs can, of course, create their own set of "opportunities." One family reports that while fix-up work was underway in the parsonage kitchen, the refrigerator was kept on the front porch. Late at night, one either had to wait for a lull in traffic or risk an exposure of evening wear in order to sneak a bedtime snack.

3. Personally, I think it would be excessive to buy more than fifteen or twenty copies of this book for the church library.

4. Where is Dr. Freud when you need him? In writing this story for me, the pastor typed "each pail of water collected had to be hauled up a *fight* of stairs."

5. One pastor says that her daughter hid in the closet during a parsonage open house. From that spot, she was able to hear numerous comments about her choice of posters and the chartreuse she had chosen for her room décor. Well, Jesus did say we should go to the closet to pray (Matthew 6:6 KJV).

6. Don't be silly. Of course I changed the name of the family and their anniversary date.

7. That's another way of saying wait until they like you before making too many changes!

6. *Guess Who's Coming to Supper (and Breakfast and Lunch)*

1. For readers of fairly recent vintage, let me explain. A clothesline is a cord or wire on which persons used to hang clothes for drying in the sunshine. The clothes were attached to the line with little springy-things called "clothespins." A clothesline did not work on a rainy day (and perhaps not on Sundays!).

2. In a few cases, you might want to put your fingers into your ears so you won't hear yourself say what you think the next words might be!

3. Ms. Holloman taught me not to end sentences in prepositions. I understand that many grammarians no longer insist on that nicety. I still get nervous about those runaway prepositions, but could not bring myself to write, *How does a pastor determine when there is something for which it is worth going to the mat?* If the preposition at the end of the sentence bothers you, I invite you to use this alternative question.

4. Everyone who disagrees with me is not an ignoramus. That basic principle can help me begin to have patience with varying points of view. What can I learn from someone (with whom I am not in accord) and what can he or she learn from me, so that both of us are stronger? A compromise is, after all, still a promise. It is a promise we both make. In contrast, recall the person who said to an opponent, "I see your point and I think if you parted your hair differently others could see it too."

5. Not his real name.

6. Not his real name either!

7. Carl Rogers developed a counseling pattern ("client-centered therapy") that was often stereotyped as quiet dialogue around the phrase "I hear you saying...." It was more

than that, of course, but my point here is that Pastor X was not quietly Rogerian at this time!

8. Our son used to say, give him ten minutes and he could find the United Methodist parsonage in any town. His view was that eventually they all began to look alike. He never reported seeing a parsonage wearing a clerical collar.

9. Unidentified parsonages in neighborhoods at some distance from the church might go pretty much unnoticed except by the immediate neighbors and by church members. Some clergy find that distance from the office to be a blessing. Some prefer the proximity to the church. Very few pastors who have a housing allowance choose to spend it on a house near the church. Think about it.

7. When Is a Gnu New?

1. More than one pastor has helped plan, make financial arrangements, and see the construction of a new parsonage just in time to move on. One colleague says, "The new house was almost completed and I was scheduled for another assignment, so three nights before we were due to leave, my family and I slipped over to the brand-new parsonage and slept in sleeping bags. We were determined to enjoy at least one night in that place even if we had to go back to the old place for breakfast!"

2. *The Book of Discipline of The United Methodist Church 2004* (Nashville: The United Methodist Publishing House, 2004), for example, has four pages of planning and financial requirements. In addition, United Methodist annual conferences often have specific parsonage standards.

3. Case in point. Should parsonage standards for furnished parsonages indicate the kind of bed the pastor ought to have? Consider this account from one pastor: "We had just moved into a new parsonage with our two boys. My wife was pregnant at the time, and we were more than a little surprised to see that every bedroom in the house was furnished with twin beds. I spoke about this to the pastor whom we were to follow, and he said, 'Well, we just pushed two of them together and it's like having a king-sized bed.'

"The first night we tried it. The mattresses were from an earlier era (the 1950s!) and rolled into the middle. The gap between the mattresses we had pushed together was like a Grand Canyon. Needless to say, we had a tough night sleeping that first night in our new parsonage.

"The next morning I went to the local hardware store to pick up a few things. After gathering up what I needed, I took them to the counter to check out. No sooner had I laid them on the counter than the man at the register asked, 'How'd you sleep last night, Preacher?' I know that news about a parsonage family can travel fast, but this was nuts!

"I replied, 'Pretty good, thanks.' The salesman smiled and asked, 'What'd you think of the bed?'

This was getting pretty personal. I said, 'Excuse me?'

" 'What'd you think of the bed? I know you've got twin beds pushed together.'

"Before I knew how to respond, an older woman came up, smiled, and asked, 'Preacher, how did you sleep last night?'

"Here I was the brand-new preacher in town, and everyone was interested in my sleeping habits and the bed my wife and I shared! As I continued to ponder what was happening, the man behind the counter said, 'Mama, the preacher needs a new bed. He and his wife don't need to push twin beds together to sleep together. The preacher needs a new bed.'

"As if I wasn't even around, the woman replied, 'Well, they can sleep in those twin beds; after all, she's already pregnant.'

"To make a long and crazy story short, by the end of the day we had a brand-new queen-sized bed with a new mattress and springs. It was absolutely beautiful, and we slept comfortably in it for the next eight years."

4. My wife, Toni, and I prefer a radically contemporary style of house. However, if we were around as a new parsonage was being built, we would not encourage that mode of building. We would have some responsibility for those without a voice: the pastors and families who will later live in that house! Does this mean that a parsonage has to be boringly ordinary? No! But it does mean that choices need to be made that will allow future occupants to have some flexibility of decorations, accessories, and furnishings in keeping with their own "flavor."

5. Consult with folks who know! One pastor tells of a new parsonage thrown together hastily by some trustees who did not check with folks who did any cooking. They made the kitchen so small that there was no place for the refrigerator. It ended up in a utility space, two rooms away.

6. The other side of the coin, of course, is the question, *Is there storage space for the parsonage items which do not fit the needs of the present parsonage family?* One pastor tells of moving into a new parsonage that was actually owned by one of the church members. The family had barely unpacked when the owner's spouse came for a visit. She went from room to room, touching each thing that was not there before, asking: "Where did you get that?" It did not occur to this pastor for years that what the visitor was actually asking was, "Where in blazes are all the beautiful plastic flower arrangements I put in here?" He notes that he could have answered that question: "They were all neatly stored, being preserved for the next parsonage family."

7. Of course, for some settings, an appropriate substitute might be a house whose screened porch faces the ocean so seagulls and breaking waves can be the only sound heard from the hammock carefully placed on the porch. These are merely suggestions, and you might need to adjust for your local circumstances.

8. In some denominations, there are procedures to be followed as a congregation builds or buys a parsonage. For example, in The United Methodist Church, certain decisions have to be made at a congregational meeting; other decisions can be made by representative groups (such as a charge conference). United Methodists should note that parsonages, as well as places of worship, are under the "trust clause," providing that title to the property is held in trust. See paragraphs 2502 and 2503 of *The Book of Discipline of The United Methodist Church 2004.* Consultation about and, in some cases, approval of building projects by denominational bodies are required. (United Methodists can look at paragraph 2543 of *The Book of Discipline of The United Methodist Church 2004.*)

9. This question moves to the edges of dreaming. Most people would like more space! The point is that if possible it really helps to have some space in the parsonage that is not so defined that future families cannot adapt it to their own circumstances. One might need a place for the father-in-law who has moved with the family; another could use a place for a sewing room. Some designs refer to this as a bonus room. It is particularly helpful in a house in which a series of families will be living!

10. This was probably a better reply than one I read somewhere: "'Shut up,' she explained."

11. Several people have told me that when they get to heaven they want to check with Noah about the inclusion on the ark of termites, fleas, mosquitoes, roaches, and ticks.

12. The chairperson of one parsonage committee writes this story: "I have always believed that when God closes a door, God opens a window. When Hurricane Isabel hit the North Carolina coast September 18, 2003, our church and parsonage were flooded. Help arrived in the form of the North Carolina Baptist Men. What a wonderful group! They moved furniture out, pulled up carpets, and cleaned. But our parsonage was condemned by the county and had to be destroyed. We were devastated. We are a small church (77 members) and funds are always low. We prayed for a solution. On January 24, we met the director of the United Methodist Marion Edwards Recovery Center Initiative. They agreed to build us a parsonage with the help of volunteers! United Methodist volunteers came from North Carolina, South Carolina, Pennsylvania, Wisconsin, and Illinois. Local people helped. There were also Baptists, Presbyterians, and several groups of Lutherans. What a blessing to see young people give up their vacation to help those in need! The landscaping was done by a teen in our community who was working on his Eagle Scout badge. We now have a beautiful parsonage, and the pastor is very happy there. The Lord has certainly blessed us!"

13. Some congregations begin companion projects when they build. A new church building is matched with funds to build a mission church in another country. A new parsonage is accompanied with a Habitat for Humanity undertaking or with support of a public housing venture.

8. View from the Pew

1. This observation is based on exhaustive research in which I asked three people what they thought. One thought the Cardinals would win the World Series. Another thought we needed rain. The third thought many pastors like the parsonage system and prefer it to a housing allowance.

2. My perception is admittedly shaped by a lifetime of parsonage living. Also, my ministry has been in a region in which parsonages are the norm for my denomination.

3. One way to do this interpretation would be to buy a copy of this book for everyone in the congregation (and their out-of-town relatives and perhaps for everyone in the same phone book). If that seems excessive, how about one copy for the church library?

4. You know by now that this is a made-up name. A friend of mine has a sister named "Faye," and a beautiful red bird just landed in a tree outside my window. That's how I came up with this name!

5. In most settings in which the same pastor serves more than one church, it seems to work best if one of the congregations owns the parsonage and the other(s) on the circuit pay rent to the church that has title. Although this arrangement clarifies maintenance issues, it has the possibility of disagreements about parsonage decisions. One way to balance these concerns is to have a parsonage committee with representatives from all the congregations involved, with majority membership from the owner church.

6. If there is an emergency plan in place (whom does the pastor contact in an emergency?) and a clear pattern of authorization (e.g., it's OK to spend up to $100 without checking with anybody) and a system of help (who is responsible for daily maintenance? landscaping? major repairs?), there are less likely to be broken places in the parsonage coordination.

7. Just to make sure we understand that the patience is a two-way street, let me share another story from the same spouse whose story generated the accolades of "how it ought to be done." She says, "I have backed my car through the garage door in three different parsonages. I replaced the doors myself, even though the church did not want me to do so. I discovered that the people in the churches we served had a lot of patience!" (I should advise anyone whom this pastor's wife will be visiting to raise the garage door before she gets there!) It was not quite a garage door, but one parsonage committee repainted the parsonage living room after our two-year-old son expressed on the wall his emerging artistic talents with crayons. Patience and generosity.

8. The same applies to people in chairs, people standing, and generally to those milling around outside the door.

9. Ten percent? If there are nine trustees and five other people on a parsonage committee, that means fourteen persons (not counting a pastoral advisory committee) are involved in parsonage thinking. That is ten percent of a 140-member church. This is pretty much the limit of my mathematical competence.

10. Some of the remarkable stories shared with me by friends who knew I was working on this book were stories of how things "used to be." I have tried to avoid using most of these accounts. They have wonderful, charming historic interest, but do not always teach us much about life in a parsonage in the twenty-first century—or do they?

9. *Last Day at the Parsonage*

1. The congregation's welcome of the new pastor does not call for you to hang around and be a part of the hospitality! I am sort of hard-nosed about not going back to former appointments, so I remind retired colleagues who still live in the community of a former church to make certain they allow plenty of space for the new pastor to get established.

2. If you are not familiar with this delicacy, call someone who has lived for at least a few years south of the Mason-Dixon Line.

3. Count the children several days in advance. You should show up at the new place with more or less the same number as you had before moving. If you have misplaced a child or two, it is awkward to continue pretending that they are at grandma's. If you have young children in the car, you will probably also have stuffed animals to which the children's arms and legs have become attached. (Those who know our family know that S. Bear always travels in the car, not on the moving truck.)

4. Confession time: in a place of service when I was still in seminary, a couple of dear sisters had asked me to be sure to stop by and see them before I left town. My visits with them in normal circumstances had been, shall we say, extended with multiple presentations of items we had discussed in previous visits. I dreaded going again. I put it off. Moving day came. Finally, I decided that I needed to salve my conscience just a little by calling them and saying that I would not have time to come by. Their phone rang. And rang. And rang. I realized they were not at home. I jumped into my car and drove directly to their home. I ran to the door and left a note indicating that I was sorry I had not seen them before leaving. I do not recommend that you follow this plan; it leaves you with almost fifty years of guilty conscience.

5. A literal translation of this text is "The Word became flesh and tented among us."

6. In traditions in which everyone in the system moves on the same day, there is almost always this quick turnaround. In other practices, there may well be days, even months,

between the Reverend Ms. Lawton and the Reverend Mr. Hansen. In fact, in some congregational settings, the pastor who is leaving will not know who the next pastor will be or when he or she will arrive.

7. Perhaps there is not another congregation waiting. Retirement (or departure from an active pastoring ministry) has its own kind of "next step" experience. As a clergyman who has been appointed to administrative ministries without a congregation, I wondered if my family and I would be on our own on moving day. In each case, I have been welcomed by new staff colleagues, community pastors, and friends who knew that "the Joyners are moving here." Often, they had even stocked the refrigerator with my favorite diet soft drink.

10. *Parsonage Prayers*

1. It is up to you whether to include the time that Uncle Edgar got so angry he slept in the car rather than continue the family discussion of politics.

2. Open house, for some, is an occasion of much joy. For others, it is unmitigated disaster waiting to happen. Christmas? (As if there is not enough going on!) Fourth of July? (As if anyone is going to be in town!) Easter? (As if you wanted to divert attention from the Resurrection!) Pastor's birthday? (As if you wanted everyone to bring presents!) One hundred-fiftieth anniversary of construction of the parsonage? (As if you actually enjoyed using the outhouse constructed in the 1750s!) April 15? (As if anyone's mind is going to be on friendly visits!) August 22? (As if you want all those people tromping through your home!) Oh, well. Any of these times will work well for persons who enjoy having an open house!

3. Department of Disclaimer: This happened fifty years ago. One pastor has remembered days when her father, also a pastor, came with the family to see the parsonage at his new work. The "tour" began with a huge puddle of water in the dining room. The cause was discovered when a visit upstairs revealed the bathroom sink lying on the floor. Her father moved in but insisted that the rest of the family stay with grandparents. The church saw massive plumbing problems and decided to build a new parsonage (no doubt without reading that chapter in this book!) and proceeded to provide an interim house.

The temporary location turned out to be a summer beach house, which was not needed in the winter. The bedrooms and the bathrooms were separated by screened porches. ("I can remember," she writes, "being carried to the bedroom when there was snow on the porches.") Summer came, and the short-term parsonage could now be rented to beach visitors so the family was trundled off to an apartment.

The apartment was quite small for the family of four. The daytime was not too bad because the two children were off at school. The evenings were a matter of close companionship and testing of family goodwill!

Then came the new parsonage. It was no fun for the young girl whose mother was terrified that sticky child handprints would mar the sparkling white walls. "Mom might have preferred living in the old house! Living was easier there!"

Thus, at least one pastor looks back at a childhood adventure and thinks, *Sometimes renovation is better on everyone!* Maybe so. Renovation might be better than living in four different houses within one year!

4. It would, I suppose, be tacky for the pastor to say, "It only took six years for anyone to care about the broken-down ceiling in the living room." And, I gather, this is not the

time for the chair of the parsonage committee to suggest, "Ever since you moved in, pastor, things seem to have gotten run-down."

5. For example, with a little reflection and creativity one could draw upon such materials as found in *The United Methodist Book of Worship* (Nashville: The United Methodist Publishing House, 1992), particularly starting on p. 610; *The Book of Common Prayer*, According to the use of The Episcopal Church, published by The Church Hymnal Corporation and Seabury Press), particularly reviewing the service beginning on p. 567 and prayers on pp. 196 and 204; *The New National Baptist Hymnal* (Nashville: National Baptist Publishing Board, 1977), particularly readings 599 and 600; *Lutheran Book of Worship* (Lutheran Church in America, The American Lutheran Church, The Evangelical Lutheran Church of Canada, and The Lutheran Church–Missouri Synod, 1978), particularly prayers on pp. 38, 39, 43, and 46; *Book of Common Worship* (Louisville: Westminster John Knox Press, 1993), particularly items 592-595; *Book of Occasional Services* (Westminster John Knox Press, 1999), particularly pp. 156-83; and *The Baptist Hymnal* (Nashville: Convention Press, 1991), particularly reading 713.

In addition to these possibilities, there are appropriate hymns in almost every hymn collection. Look in the topical index under Home, Family, and Church, or similar headings to find selections.

6. Alas and alack, my foolish mind has raced to the possibilities of a series of liturgical dances developed specifically around dodging sawhorses, avoiding falling scaffolding, and picking up one's foot quickly upon stepping on an errant nail. Perhaps it is better to make certain that construction will be completed before setting the date of the special service!

7. How would you like for fifty strangers to show up at your house saying they have come to deconsecrate it?

8. Hmm. "When we lived here, the furnace never worked and we almost froze." Response: "God has been here. Thanks be to God."

11. In Conclusion

1. The implication of this observation is that this book will have historic value long after it has lost its practical value. You may want to rush out and buy another dozen copies to leave to your great-grandchildren.

2. If it always worked, some of the stories in this book would be a lot less interesting!

3. Some denominational politues have procedures for intervention ministries in those cases in which congregation and pastor cannot come to shared understandings.

4. If there is no "neutral" party to lend a hand in times of a parsonage crisis, consider using these questions as the agenda for a meeting of appropriate local church officials.

5. Because I have changed the names of pastors, I have also changed the names of congregations!

6. As it happens, I was district superintendent of the churches described in this story. I have been in the parsonage. It was a small frame house, unpretentious in every way. Most of its furnishings had served several pastoral families. It was located downwind from the exhaust fans of a major restaurant. But there is nothing of complaint in this pastor's report. All of those seeming limitations are put into perspective by the love the people had for their pastor. She returned the love in kind.

7. The full story is a bit more than can be told here, but suffice it to say it includes a white cat that became jet black, smoke spewing throughout the house, and rooms that looked like the smoking section of a tobacco convention.